S0-BUD-042

Welcome to the Middle East
Book 1

ALISS - ACTIVE LEARNING IN SOCIAL SCIENCE

Editor	Gretchen Winkleman
Project Director	John Minkler
	Yosemite High School District

Writing Team

Lisa Bartels-Rabusin
Fresno Unified School District

Mollie Macmullin
Coarsegold Union School District

Sarajayne Gazarian
Fresno Unified School District

Lydia Monk
Coarsegold Union School District

Sandra GilpinBlack
Fresno Unified School District

Zandra Milfs Ogata
Fresno Unified School District

Robert Jost
Fresno Unified School District

Ann Williamson
Fresno Unified School District

Sara M. Kelly
Corcoran Unified School District

Donald Wilson
Merced City School District

Illustrator	Philip Brewer
Contributing Artists	Gary Tellez, Cristel Andresen Werner

 Fresno Pacific College

Fresno Pacific College is a Christian, liberal-arts college, affiliated with the Mennonite Brethren Church. The College is accredited by the Western Association of Schools and Colleges. The campus is located at 1717 South Chestnut Street, Fresno California 93702. This book has been written and published under the auspices of the Professional Development Division, which provides in-service education courses in a variety of subjects and current topics. Readers are invited to write, call (209) 453-2015, or fax (209) 453-2006 for full information.

Copyright © 1994 by Fresno Pacific College. All rights reserved. The owner of this book is automatically given a copyright waiver to copy any number of student pages for his or her own classroom use. Copying any other portion of the contents or distributing copies of student pages to others will be considered an infringement of the legal copyright protection. Brief passages may be used in reviews or references. Any exception to this arrangement must be by written agreement with the publisher. Royalties from the sale of this publication will be used for the work of the Professional Development Division in producing similar materials and enriching the skills of teachers throughout the world.

Printed in the United States of America
Layout and design by John Lopes, Graphic Design Department, Fresno Pacific College
Cover credits:
    Featured photograph by Gretchen Winkleman
    Other photographs courtesy of Aramco World
    Design by John Lopes

ISBN 1-884397-00-X

Table of Contents

Dear Educators,

Social science is intended to prepare students for the responsibilities of citizenship in an increasingly complex world.

A group of teachers in grades five through ten was convened by the Professional Development (PD) Division of Fresno Pacific College to discuss how they could help. These teachers wanted action and were willing to commit time and energy to a workable solution, whatever that might be. When they analyzed what seemed to be successful in their own classrooms, they found that the common thread was thought-provoking activity.

Those teaching in self-contained elementary classrooms found that the subjects in which there was more activity were the more popular subjects; the subjects in which—for whatever reason—instruction was more textbook-oriented were considered uninteresting and even boring. Teachers of social studies in middle schools or junior high schools admitted that instruction on those levels tended to be less active; they agreed that when they involved the students in something more than textbook discussion, interest in the specific subject under consideration rose noticeably. Field trips, for example, were the high points of the year. Activity, then, was a crucial element.

Next, the group discussed how the importance of student participation in social science could best be communicated to other teachers. They concluded that they could gather together activities which they had found successful in their own classrooms; if they could do it, others could, too. They committed to passing along some active social science activities. They became a writing team.

While these discussions were taking place, the Gulf War broke out. The writing team realized that in their own classrooms they were discarding their planned curricula to help students gain an understanding of the Middle East. In so doing, they found that students knew next to nothing about that part of the world. If this was true in California, where the Middle East is an official part of the social science curriculum, students in other parts of the country probably knew even less. They determined that they would publish activities focused on the Middle East, past and present. The PD administration agreed to sponsor the project, and nearly three years later, you have the result in your hands.

Here are the essential elements of the ALISS program:

1. Active, hands-on learning
2. An appreciation for how our own cultural heritage has come from people who lived in other times and other parts of the world
3. A recognition that people who live in other places with other lifestyles are human beings with many of the same needs that we have
4. An increased awareness of international current events and their implications
5. The identification of individual and social values that form the foundation of a responsible and productive society
6. The increased awareness of the individual's responsibility to participate in social problem solving, from interpersonal to global levels
7. The distinction between people's present and past lifestyles, so that inaccurate stereotypes are dispelled.

The materials in this book incorporate these elements. Because our world is constantly changing, we have tried to balance the past and present. Students need to know cognitive material about their heritage from the historical past, but they must also gain skills which will help them process the ever-changing world situation. Beyond this, they need to be concerned about the world and its ever-present problems; they need to care what happens, not only to themselves but to people with problems of many kinds thoughtout the world. Only by this combination of (1) knowing the facts, (2) gaining the skills for processing information, and (3) adopting a caring attitude will students become responsible citizens who are actively and appropriately involved in their personal futures and the future of the communities of the world.

On behalf of the Professional Development Division and also Fresno Pacific College, I am pleased to present this first book on the Middle East, the results of almost three years of work. I commend the writing team members for their contributions to this publication.

May you, as teachers, find the material presented here useful in your classroom.

Anita Andresen

Anita L. Andresen
Dean, Professional Development Division
Fresno Pacific College

January, 1994

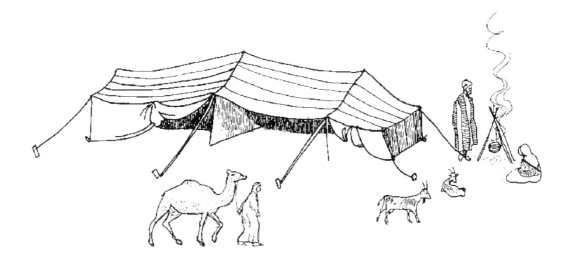

We gratefully acknowledge the contributions made by the following:

Diane Winkleman Bennett	Resource, culture
Bonnie Trask (Fresno City College)	Resource, history
Suzanne LeRoux (Department of Defense Schools, Bahrain) .	Resource, culture
Carole Bekat (Department of Defense Schools, Turkey) . .	Resource, culture
Cristel Andresen Werner	Computer graphics
Many teachers throughout central California, especially Jon Moskowitz, and Ruthanne Sena (Kerman Unified School District)	Field testing
Aramco Oil Services, especially John Arndt and Lee Vinzant .	Resource, photos
Tiffney & Timothy Kazarian Kuckenbaker	Cover models

1   Deciding Which Countries to Include

The term *Middle East* means different things to different people. To some, it is a group of countries most of whose people speak Arabic. To others it is the source of most of the petroleum used by the rest of the world. Still others know only a few facts they may have learned during the latest Middle East crisis. In the United States these limited perceptions may be due to the fact that our language and most of our cultural heritage is rooted in western Europe. The ALISS program has tried to build a more complete knowledge base. Consequently, an early task was to develop a list of countries for which we would provide activities and other resources.

Historical Background

It is helpful to look back at the region's early known history, with the ancient herders grazing their flocks along the valleys of the Tigris and Euphrates Rivers. In ancient times this region was known as the *Land Of Five Seas* and *the middle of the earth*. Traders and conquerors traveling between Europe and Africa or Europe and Asia passed through this area. Europeans came to think of this region as the gateway to the Far East; as a result they began referring to it as the *Near East*.

The use of the term *Middle East* is comparatively recent. In 1902, Alfred Thayer Mahan, American naval historian, is known to have used it in referring to the strategic naval area between Arabia and India, around the Persian Gulf and eastward from there. Soon the British government started using the term officially in their documents. Because so many have considered the term appropriate, it has been used extensively since that time.

Similarities and Differences

Among Westerners who have at least a basic knowledge of the Middle East, most would agree that it includes Saudi Arabia and the other countries on the Arabian peninsula. In these countries the people have a similar appearance, including skin color and facial features. These people share a common language (Arabic), a common faith (Islam), and similar economic and political interests based mainly on the discovery and development of extensive petroleum resources. The land is much the same—narrow strips of fertile coastline bordering a dry inland desert.

Most lists of Middle East countries would add the neighboring countries of Iran, Iraq, Syria, Lebanon, Jordan, and Israel. Actually these countries are considered the heart of the Middle East because it was across this area that explorers, traders, and conquerors established their travel routes. Within this region lies what is referred to as the *Fertile Crescent*. While there are many similarities between these countries and those on the Arabian Peninsula (geography, religion, culture), the comparison of any one of these countries to the Arabian Peninsula shows differences: for example, Israel is similar in geography but includes many Jewish people with a religion and a language which is different. Traveling east and north, the variety continues. In our quest for a "master list", it does not help that different world organizations include different lists of countries: the *National Geographic Society* includes Sudan and Turkey in their 1991 map of the Middle East, while many Middle East and Arab organizations exclude Iran and Turkey from their lists. Many maps and lists include all of northern Africa.

How Big is the Middle East?

Because authorities differ, answering this question was no easy task. ALISS writers wanted to be accurate, yet practical. If the list of countries was too long, teachers and students might become overwhelmed and discouraged. If the list was too short, on the other hand, they might oversimplify the complexities of the area, complexities which are important on the world's scene.

We began by listing all of the countries and territories that any reliable sources placed on maps or lists specifically labeled *Middle East*:

Afghanistan	Gaza Strip	Qatar
Algeria	Golan Heights	Saudi Arabia
Bahrain	West Bank	Sudan
Cyprus	Jordan	Syria
Egypt	Kuwait	Tunisia
Ethiopia	Lebanon	Turkey
Iran	Libya	United Arab Emirates
Iraq	Morocco	Yemen
Israel	Oman	

Note that this list includes the occupied or disputed territories of Golan Heights, West Bank, and the Gaza Strip. Geographically these are part of the area; although they are not countries in the diplomatic sense, a recognition of their existence is necessary to an understanding of the dynamics of the region.

Since it was felt that this list was too long to be practical, our next decision was to eliminate from our list any country considered a part of the continents of Asia, Africa, or Europe. The Middle East, or the Near East as it was called earlier, was a trade route, and as such was really the route by which people from Africa and Europe reached the Far East or Orient. Afghanistan is sometimes included in a list of Middle East countries, but mainly because it is part of the Arab World. Although Egypt and other countries of northern Africa are sometimes included on various maps and lists, it was felt that for our purposes, these countries would best be covered in a separate study of Africa as a continent. (You would be in good company if you chose to place Egypt on the final list, since it has had a great influence on the historical and cultural development of the Middle East!) Cyprus was eliminated because of its strong ties to Greece and the complex political issues which a study of it would raise.

There is a realistic limit to what a unit on the Middle East can accomplish. At any rate, these countries and territories remained:

Bahrain	Kuwait
Iran	Lebanon
Iraq	Oman
Israel	Qatar
Occupied Territories:	Saudi Arabia
Golan Heights	Syria
Gaza Strip	Turkey
West Bank	United Arab Emirates
Jordan	Yemen

If at all possible, students should study all of the countries and territories, so that they will have at least an initial appreciation for all of the people of the Middle East. Since Egypt has had such an enormous influence on the history of the area, it is hoped that teachers will find time to include more than a brief mention of it, especially if the local curriculum does not include the study of Egypt separately.

2   Skills and Strategies

Elementary and middle school teachers who use a variety of appropriate teaching methods provide for their students an exciting environment for learning. In this chapter, and in the ALISS program as a whole, we seek to supplement whatever background in teaching strategies that you, as teachers, have to offer. Here are a few notes on the various approaches that may be useful in active social science.

Important Social Science Skills

Dialogue

When two people talk, they may or may not be having a dialogue. Dialogue is true, open communication, in which both participants have a questioning attitude and a willingness to learn about the topic under discussion.

One way to understand the importance of proper dialogue is to examine an analogy using three general levels of reading or listening skills. At the lowest comprehension level, students look for <u>facts and answers</u>; if they have memorized the right ones, they feel they have an understanding of a topic. In years past, the goal of education was to fill students full of facts. On this level, the communication was between the teacher and each individual student, the teacher asking the question and the student answering.

The next higher level of reading comprehension would include skills like <u>drawing conclusions and making inferences</u>. With these a student would learn facts and examine them but would also seek legitimate, unstated conclusions which might reasonably be based on the facts given. For example, if I say it is cold outside and the ground is gradually becoming white, you could reasonably infer that it is snowing. Some thinking is required to decide what conclusions and inferences are legitimate from the given facts, and along with communication between the teacher and individual students, there might also be discussion between or among students to determine whether or not a given conclusion is a reasonable one.

The highest level of reading or listening comprehension is the <u>creative thinking</u> level, in which students exercise analytical thinking and critical judgment. They use the factual and inferential levels, to be sure, but they exercise problem-solving creativity with thinking patterns that are not predetermined. On this level, much more of the communication is apt to be between (or among) students as they examine multiple perspectives, value systems, and changing conditions in which any solutions will need to be applied. On this level, students use skills acquired on the two lower levels to examine the issues, form preliminary opinions, and then share findings and questions. The search is for broad conclusions and solutions to which most students in the group will agree.

It is the communication among teacher(s) and students on this highest comprehension level that constitute dialogue. One student's conclusions may be based on limited information or faulty reasoning. Another's value system may be called into question by other students. As various viewpoints are shared, the pool of information grows along with the emotional involvement of participants. As a result, discussion during dialogue may become heated, and teachers usually find that students continue to discuss issues outside of the classroom. This is healthy because it shows that students are relating these issues to their everyday lives.

Training students to dialogue is the key to developing students with responsible opinions on social issues. They need lots of guidance and practice, and they learn to ask questions as they learn to listen to the answers, especially when the issue is controversial.

To achieve an atmosphere in class in which students are assertively participating in these dialogues, you need to set some ground rules. Students need to feel safe about expressing an opinion with which others may disagree. There must be some agreement about respect for each person's point of view, and students will need to disagree without using put-downs. Students also need to feel that you respect, encourage, and even reward the expression of diverse views. In some cases you may also need to have an agreement on the appropriateness of responses, such as a restriction against suggestions that involve hurting innocent people. Agree upon a one-word signal to stop the action at any time.

Eventually students who participate in dialogue should develop a number of skills. They should listen more attentively to the opinions expressed by others. They should also learn to improve the quality of the questions they ask. Most importantly, they should refine their ability to express a reasoned opinion based on adequate information.

Critical thinking and dialogue raise a student's self-concept:

> *When the teacher encourages me to express an opinion and I am treated with respect, I feel good.*

> *Sometimes after I have shared an idea and my classmates have asked me questions about it, I realize that it wasn't a very good idea. I'm glad no one made fun of me. The next time I'll make sure I have my facts straight!*

> *The last time I said what I thought, someone said, "Oh, I never thought of it that way." That made me feel really important.*

To encourage critical thinking, we need to start by taking time to listen to the opinions our students are expressing during social science discussions. Oddly enough, many find that the seeds of critical thinking were there, in our classrooms, all the time. We are simply taking seriously the comments — and the dialogue — we tended to ignore before.

Asking Good Questions

Questioning is an art which has been valued in education for centuries. Teachers have found that when just the right question is asked in just the right way, students are challenged to think and answer in a way that helps them to learn and grow in a very special way.

In ALISS, we believe that participation includes asking good questions. As teachers, we need to model the questioning attitude and show students that questions are excellent tools to use in finding and analyzing available information. Here are some pointers on forming and asking good questions:

- Use questions to help students picture a situation. Build question upon question to dig out all of the facts they will need to understand it.
- Follow up factual (or yes-no) questions with questions that ask how or why the fact is true. These questions force students to defend what they say and to think before they speak.
- Ask questions that focus on the history or background of a problem.
- Have students practice writing and asking questions in a session where you concentrate on what constitutes a good question. Have students make up questions to be used on a test.
- When a discussion degenerates into an emotional argument, defuse the situation by asking questions that help students return to the facts.
- Ask questions on all three comprehension levels described above in the *Dialogue* section.

Achieving and Maintaining the Right Atmosphere

Most teachers who use the skills and strategies outlined in this chapter and applied throughout this book find themselves discussing topics that are increasingly controversial. The reason seems to be that instinctively they realize that the students are capable of discussing and forming judgments on more and more complicated issues.

As the topics become more controversial, it becomes increasingly important to control the emotional involvement of the students. It helps if some basic principles are in place. A discussion in one classroom (taking a whole class period) produced the following guidelines:

1. I want to feel safe and respected when I express an opinion, even if I am the only one holding that view.
2. I will respect each person's point of view.
3. In disagreeing, I will commend the other person for <u>something</u> before asking a question or making a statement by

which I continue the process of seeking truth.

4. It is good for us to have diverse views. If we agreed all the time on everything, life would be boring.
5. It will not be acceptable to express a view that would involve the hurting of innocent people.

How to post and maintain these will vary from one situation to another. All we are saying is that it is well worth the time to develop such guidelines.

Discussing Unresolved Issues

In social science classes there will be discussions on many issues that may never be resolved. This is no reason to avoid such topics; it can be very profitable to examine why the issue is so difficult. Furthermore, students need to learn that in real life, issues are not tied in neat little units with a solution at the end of each chapter. At the time of publication, the status of Palestinians is a prime example of such an issue. Even though students are frustrated when they find out how long this issue has remained unresolved and how deep the hostilities between Israelis and Palestinians lie, it is still a good topic to research and examine. When students reach the conclusion that an issue is so complex that it may never be resolved, they learn some supreme lessons: they feel some of the pain through which such peoples go and realize the need for continued work toward a solution.

Specific Strategies to Use

Simulations

A simulation is an attempt to recreate someone else's (or something else's) experience, an experience which would otherwise have been impossible. In social science, simulations are useful for recreating historical or cultural events of the past or present; imaginary simulations are also useful. They develop what is sometimes called *historical empathy*. By being placed in those circumstances, they realize that at that time (whether past, present, or imaginary) the people involved would not know what was for them the future.

In a simulation, students are assigned roles and given information essential for those roles. Then they are presented with a task or an open-ended problem. They are expected to perform the task or solve the problem in a manner consistent with their roles. As the simulation progresses, they will need group discussions and other indicators of the consequences of their actions along the way. By being placed in a situation with a realistic structure, students can gain experience in higher levels of thinking, forming critical judgments and making decisions regarding the situation in which they find themselves.

The goal of a simulation is to help the learner identify emotionally with the person who actually faces that problem in real life. By playing the role of a starving person in the desert, for example, a student must think of alternatives, only to find that none are live options. The simplistic thinking gives way to an emotional impact and the student is ready to discuss the consequences of hunger in the world.

Almost any social science situation is appropriate for simulations. If there is a school-wide problem of some sort, you might begin by having students adopt the roles of principal, teachers, and students with differing views on the issue. Instead of involving everyone in the class the first time, try using several outgoing students to model the strategy; then you can choose a simulation with an issue related to your current social science curriculum. With proper briefing and encouragement, students will usually assume their roles and gradually respond to the situation. For some less able students, there may need to be a student/partner who acts as coach and resource.

Sometimes strong feelings arise, especially when students perceive a situation to be unfair. The key is to create an atmosphere in which students feel comfortable sharing their feelings and resolving conflicts with mutual respect.

For simulations to be successful,

- Be sure students know their roles and what is expected of them before you begin.
- Talk with students beforehand about staying in their roles during the activity. If they have trouble doing this during the simulation, give reminders such as information about the historical period or the point of view that they represent.
- Beforehand, set up a time-out rule so that, if necessary, you can stop the action and get back on track.

Simulations can be especially exciting when students do not know the actual (historical) outcome of a situation. After you have finished the simulation, it is especially important to discuss what happened and why. This is where the students will synthesize—and usually moderate—their previous views.

Readers' Theater

Another way to get students to learn other points of view is to have them participate in a dramatic presentation. *Readers' Theater* differs from simulations in that the emphasis is on the action *before* the drama rather than *during* it. The most effective readers' theaters are those in which students write the dramas, although it is also possible to use dramas written by someone else. Often after doing a readers' theater with a prepared script, students are willing to write their own. Again, an important element is the subsequent discussions of the dramas and their implications. Especially if there are unresolved issues after a readers' theater, you may want to follow it with a simulation to help students moderate their opposing views.

Cooperative Learning Groups

Having students work in small groups keeps on-task behavior and motivation high. The basic procedure is to divide the class into small groups, assign the task(s), and monitor the progress. Each student and each group is accountable to peers for completing the assigned task. As a result, several things seem to happen:

- Students stay on-task a larger percentage of the instructional time.
- Thinking and work produced is at a higher level than many of the students would have been able to achieve individually.
- In addition to lower level comprehension skills like finding facts and defining terms, students use higher-level skills like questioning generalizations and looking for assumptions.
- Students develop an increased respect for contributions of students often considered less able or less acceptable because of some factor such as race, sex, culture, language, or academic ability.
- Several groups cover a larger quantity of material than one large group (such as a class) could cover in the same time.
- High motivation results in students often continuing their discussions and work beyond class time, even when this is not required.
- Students learn many social skills, such as really listening to one another and compromising.
- Racial and other inter-group relationships improve because students tend to forget these differences as they work together.

To implement cooperative learning, you should first choose an appropriate topic with one task or a group of parallel tasks. When you begin, you are actually teaching students how to operate in small groups; using the same topic for all groups is often a good way to do this while maintaining control. In most cooperative activities there should be some way of reporting results: an activity sheet, transparency, or a project. In preparing this, be sure that directions are complete, so that group members will not spend time arguing about the procedure. (The higher the reading level of your group, the more of the directions you can include in writing.) The activity sheet should help groups to gather information they will find helpful in the culminating session.

Plan beforehand how you will divide the students into groups. First, decide how many groups you will have. Then assign a strong student to each group. Next, assign the weakest students. Now distribute the other students to all groups. Lastly, adjust assignments to make sure they are balanced according to sex, ethnic composition, and compatibility. Avoid assigning best friends or worst enemies to the same group.

Give the class any general background information, along with any directions not included in a written worksheet and an indication of the time schedule. Check that everyone understands what is to be done and how; this is often assumed but is actually the cause of a great many difficulties.

Explain to groups how they should assign roles within each group, by students volunteering, drawing slips of paper, or some other method. Here are the roles we recommend for groups of five:

- The **facilitator** helps the group meet its goals, not by making all of the decisions or telling group members what to do, but by making comments about the group's progress and asking questions which will help the group stay focussed on its task.
- The **timer** helps the group plan and use its time properly on various parts of the task and then monitors the work time left to reach assigned goals. This person may also be expected to get and return necessary supplies for the task.
- The **reporter** records required information and helpful notes during the activity and then shares the group's findings and questions in the final whole-class discussion.
- The **encourager** watches the group work and makes notes about (only) the positive things said and done during group work.

Especially the first time you use cooperative learning groups with a class, you may want to place small signs with these role explanations on all group tables, so that all students will be reminded of their roles during the group work time.

As groups work, circulate as a resource to encourage them and keep them on task. Be especially careful to praise students who are productive and cooperative. Intervene to correct inappropriate behaviors as they occur.

The culmination of the activity is a whole-class discussion in which groups share what they have done. If all groups complete the same task, this summary discussion will be an opportunity to sharing findings that are somewhat similar and discuss the reasons for any differences; the advantage here is that you can easily see and deal with how well groups followed directions. When using varied tasks, you should allow more time for this final phase, because each group is really teaching the rest of the class what they did and what they learned; because students tend to become more involved emotionally than in traditional settings, they will be frustrated if they do not have an opportunity to share what they have done.

Groups of three or four seem to work best. Often the roles of reporter and encourager can be combined, but never omit the role of encourager altogether. This role is crucial if you want to improve the cooperative group work of your class; by rewarding positively the behaviors that are on-task and productive, you will do much to encourage the repetition of those same behaviors. Often the size of your groups will depend on the requirement of a particular activity or the total number of groups that are desirable for a given topic. An example is the activity *Which Countries Are in the Middle East* in this book; unless you have time to cover the whole list of countries by repeating the activity at least once, it will be necessary to have groups for as many as possible of the countries viewed by the rest of the world as the most influential in the region.

Cooperative groups are excellent for a number of activities. To review a section in any subject, divide into groups and have each group make up several questions. Then they take turns asking the rest of the class the questions. Keep score or not, as you wish.

Teachers consider the assigning of grades the most difficult part of using cooperative learning groups. This factor should not be used to discount the tremendous value of the groups; it only means you must find an arrangement that works for you. Structure grades to encourage all group members to help one another, not just do the best they can individually. Decide on a list of individual and group behaviors/outcomes that you consider valuable; make up a chart listing them, and use the chart to evaluate each person. Here are some other ideas teachers have found useful:

- Assign the same grade to everyone in a group.
- Give each group member a score; then average these and give this average score to every member of that group.
- Grant an individual score plus a group bonus if all members achieve a certain level.
- Give all group members the lowest member's score; although group members do not like this strategy, it does result in the group recognizing and helping the lowest members.
- Assign two scores for each group, an average academic score plus one for cooperative effort; all group members get this score.
- Assign an average score to everyone in a group, and then raise or lower this for observed work and behavior.

Whatever strategy you choose, be sure to announce your standards beforehand, so they really do motivate students.

Jigsaw

This is a fast way to synthesize a large amount of information. Choose a topic in which several different segments can be subdivided into the same subtopics. An example would be choosing the same five topics (like crops, natural resources, climate, and so on) within seven countries of a region. In this illustration, students meet in seven *home groups*, with each group studying a different country. They count off and then regroup in *expert groups* according to those numbers, with all ones together and so on.

In each expert group, material on a specific topic is distributed and discussed. For example, one group might study the status of women, while another might study the importance of oil production. In these expert groups, members read their sections silently, discuss it, or cover the material however you decide. They discuss what they have read and identify important ideas. Then, these students return to their home groups, where they would share how they think that topic is related to the country that the home group is studying. Since each group member has participated in an expert group, each one will be able to contribute to the home group. In this way, all members of each home group are exposed to all information.

Jigsaw is an excellent strategy to use in helping students to realize the importance of good reading skills. Distributing reading materials and expecting students to read and understand them may seem like a dry exercise, but it also affords opportunities to improve comprehension skills by discussing how they should find the main idea in a newspaper clipping or how they would illustrate a particular situation.

Pyramid Method

This is a way for students to plan and write an oral or written report; it is useful for students of all ages, including adults. Skip this section until you have about twenty minutes to really work through one application.

To do it properly you need a piece of shelf paper, standard width and 20 to 24 inches long. You may also use three pieces of standard copy paper, taped together side by side. For this application, you may want to outline a college paper you are working on or an upcoming speech. Work it through yourself before trying it with students.

Place the shelf paper on your desk the long way. At the top center draw a horizontal line, and on this line write the topic on which you are reporting. From the middle of this line draw three lines downward as shown. (Now you know how the strategy got its name!) Draw a horizontal line under each of these three lines.

At this point you or the students need to be reminded of the question words: *who, what, when, where, why, and how.* If necessary write them up in the corner of the chart. On the left-hand horizontal line write—or think of—a question using one question word and your topic. Then answer the first question, as shown below.

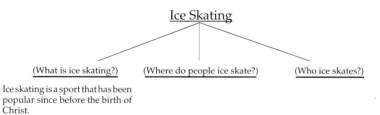

Under the first answer (above), draw three more lines to form a smaller pyramid. Under each line draw a horizontal line, as before. On these three lines write three sentences that explain or illustrate the general statement. Do this also for the other two question words. An example of this part is given on page fifteen.

Now look back at the first small pyramid ("What . . .") with its one general sentence and the three sentences under it. Together these four sentences form a perfect paragraph. The first is the topic paragraph, and all of the others tell about it. If students—or you—write this way, you will never be criticized for having sentences in a paragraph that do not belong.

You can always go back and change any part of the structure; that is the advantage of using the large worksheet until you are ready to copy your paragraphs and edit them. There is something about being able to scan horizontally and see the "big picture" that really empowers writers of all ages. In one junior high school in Indiana a substitute teacher used it, and before the day was out she had been asked for permission to use it by the librarian, two English teachers, and the reading teacher. It works!

If you had been asked to write a one-page report and if you had done all three small pyramids, you would have finished the rough draft of your report at this point. All you would need to do is copy the three paragraphs in narrative paragraph form and edit them.

If you want a longer report, start the same way. Form your three small pyramids first. Then use each of the three sentences (such as the three under "What...") as the topic sentence for another paragraph. In this way, there would be a total of three paragraphs (nine sentences) under "What..." and a total of nine paragraphs under the three question words.

You don't have to have three branches to the original pyramid: you can have five, or two, or whatever number you wish. Three seems to be a good number to start with. Also, you may want to assign the question words or phrases to be used: in a book report you might have branches for (1) the setting, (2) the characters, (3) the plot, and (4) your opinion of the book.

Work on the large paper(s) as long as you can, even if you have to write small in the corners. Make the pyramids work for you until you are sure you have your report well developed. Then copy it in paragraph form.

Now the editing begins; read through it, preferably aloud. Should you add an introduction or a summary? Do the sentences flow smoothly? Are there words that don't quite express your thoughts? Do you need to verify any facts you mention?

Remember that as you use your worksheet, you can go back and change any topics or sentences you wish. The joy will be realizing that when you have finished outlining your topic, you have completed most of the work in an efficient and well-organized manner. When you teach this strategy, you are providing a skill that is easy to remember and useful throughout life.

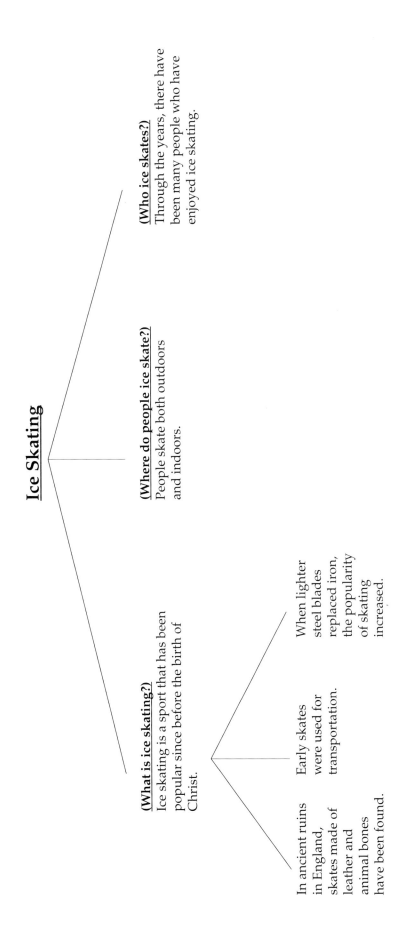

Ice Skating

(Who ice skates?)
Through the years, there have been many people who have enjoyed ice skating.

(Where do people ice skate?)
People skate both outdoors and indoors.

(What is ice skating?)
Ice skating is a sport that has been popular since before the birth of Christ.

In ancient ruins in England, skates made of leather and animal bones have been found.

Early skates were used for transportation.

When lighter steel blades replaced iron, the popularity of skating increased.

3   What do you know about the Middle East?

1.   Where is the Middle East?

2.   Name 4 countries in the Middle East.

3.   Name something we use that comes from there.

4.   What is the weather like?

5.   Name some foods the people eat.

6.   What languages do people speak there?

7.   What religion do the people follow?

8.   Has the MIddle East been in the news recently? Explain.

9.   Does the Middle East have anything to do with world peace?

10. Can you name anyone who lives in the Middle East?

[This survey may be used as pretest and/or posttest for your study of the Middle East.]

4 Visitors From the Middle East

Focus

A readers' theater will introduce this area of study with two female visitors in traditional and modern clothing.

Resources

wall map of the Middle East
optional: clothing (see Teaching Tips)

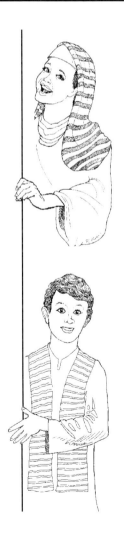

Teaching Tips

1. Beforehand,
   - Choose 4 students for visitors and interviewers.
   - Clothe visitors. Visitor 1 wears a knee-length, plain-colored (dark or dull), long-sleeved dress, with slacks under it, dark socks, and sandals. She carries a wool or cotton, 36-inch square scarf. Visitor 2 wears a jeans or other simple skirt, short-sleeved blouse, white socks, and flat shoes.
   - Fill in the blanks in the scripts, and be sure the visitors can pronounce their own names.

2. This readers' theatre should be presented in a spontaneous manner. Do not try to answer all questions; you want to raise questions and arouse interest.

Try This

Distribute scripts to all students and have them take turns reading all parts.

Script 1 - Visitors From the Middle East

Visitor 1: (knocks on the door) Excuse me. I was told to report to this classroom.

Interviewer 1: Come in. Welcome. A few of us knew that we were going to have a visit from someone from the Middle East. I assume you are our exchange student.

Visitor 1: Yes, my name is Jawazi (Jah - **wah** - zee). I am from Jordan.

Interviewer 1: This is wonderful. Our class is just starting to study the Middle East. Perhaps you can help us.

Visitor 1: I would be most happy to. Would you like me to show you my home on the map?

Interviewer 1: That would be great.

Visitor 1: *(They go to the map . She points to an area in rural, northwestern Jordan.)* Here is where my home is. I live in a small town in the Hasemite Kingdom of Jordan.

Interviewer 1: Do all of the women in your town dress as you are?

Visitor 1: Most of the girls in my town dress like this. We wear slacks under our dresses in the cold weather for warmth. My family is traditional, what you would call old-fashioned. When I get married, I will wear a scarf like this (folds scarf in half diagonally and puts it around her head), but I will only wear a veil (holds the end of the scarf across face below her eyes) when there are strangers around.

Interviewer 1: Tell us about where you live.

Visitor 1: We live in a small village, in a flat-roofed house made of stone. My father herds sheep and plants a small field of wheat. We also have some fig and olive trees.

Interviewer 1: What about the rest of your family?

Visitor 1: I have three brothers and four sisters. We used to be nomads, traveling all the time to find grazing lands for our sheep, but now we live in the village. When I was little, I had to stay home and help my mother with the younger children. Now things are changing, and we all go to school.

Interviewer 1: Do your mother and father miss having the help at home?

Visitor 1: They certainly do. My father misses having the boys to help with the farm work and my mother says I was good with the younger children. But they are glad we are getting an education.

Interviewer 1: We have a lot more questions we would like to ask, Jawazi, but our time is up. Thank you for your visit.

Visitor 1: (She bows her head and leaves.)

Script 2 - Visitors From the Middle East

Visitor 2: (Peeks in the doorway) Pardon, is this Mr./Ms._____'s room?

Interviewer 2: Yes, come in. Welcome to our classroom and to our country.

Visitor 2: Thank you. My name is Etel (Et - **tell**). I come from the city of Damascus in the country of Syria. Here, I'll show you on the map. (She does so.)

Interviewer 2: Thank you. Now tell us how large Damascus is.

Visitor 2: Damascus has more people than Detroit. The population was about 1,400,000 in 1991.

Interviewer 2: Do you go to school?

Visitor 2: Oh yes, every day, just as I understand you do here. My older sister attends the university.

Interviewer 2: Good. What do your parents do?

Visitor 2: My father owns a store and sells fruits and vegetables. My mother works with him, and we children help too, when we are not in school. My mother and father grew up on farms outside the city. Now we live right in the city and sell what someone else has grown.

Interviewer 2: Can women hold important jobs in Syria?

Visitor 2: The number of women who become doctors, lawyers, and important business executives is growing, but very, very slowly. It is really still a man's world there. In many Middle East countries it is against the law for women to hold important positions. In some countries, women cannot even drive their own cars.

Interviewer 2: Does everyone in Damascus wear western-style clothes like you have on?

Visitor 2: No, most do, but older people and those that live outside of the city wear traditional clothes. They like to come into the city to shop and visit friends.

Interviewer 2: I want to thank you for visiting us. We know there is much more to learn about the Middle East.

Visitor 2: That is right. Our part of the world is often called the Cradle of Civilization because our history goes back many, many centuries. I am proud of my country and our ways, just as you are proud of yours. Thank you for letting me visit your class. Have a good time studying the Middle East. I wish you well. (She bows her head and exits.)

5   Which Countries Are in the Middle East?

Focus

Students learn about countries of the Middle East by making posters in cooperative learning groups.

Resources

Part 1 (for the class): (See Chapter 22 for maps.)
5 transparencies of map *The Mediterranean Region*
1 transparency of map *The Ottoman Empire*
transparency pens
overhead projector

Part 2:
For each student:
   outline map of country(ies) to be studied for
      each group,
   outline of the map Middle East
For the class:
   Middle East with geographical features (geo-
      physical map)
   transparency of list of countries

Part 3 (for each group):
Poster board
Colored markers
Meter sticks or yardsticks for straight edges
World maps or globe
Encyclopedias and other resource books with
   other information such as flags
Transparency of 1 of the resource sheets

Background

See Chapter 1, *Deciding Which Countries Should Be Included.*

Teaching Tips

1. To explain what countries will be studied as part of the Middle East unit you will build layers of transparencies on the overhead in *Part 1*, coloring each with something one group of the countries have in common. The goal of this part of the activity is to help students understand the complexity of what seems to be a simple task, naming the countries of the Middle East. It should have the added benefit of preparing them for reading different lists of countries in different sources. In *Part 2* they will divide into cooperative learning groups, with each group learning about one country and making a poster incorporating the information. In *Part 3* each group will present the information learned to the rest of the class by presenting and explaining the poster.

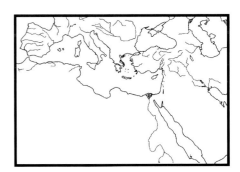

The Mediterranean Region

2. Beforehand, update information on resource sheets using newspapers, newsmagazines, or a current world almanac. *Optional: Use a transparency of the list of countries to help groups choose which country they will use for a poster.*

3. Add other transparencies with other common elements. See Chapter 22 for maps.

Procedure

Part 1 Defining the region

1. Place one transparency on the overhead projector. Color with one color the countries in which most of the people speak Arabic: Morocco, Libya, Tunisia, Libya, Egypt, and Sudan; Sinai Peninsula, all of the Arabian peninsula, Jordan, Syria, Lebanon, West Bank, the Gaza Strip, Iraq , and Kuwait. Note you are omitting Turkey, Israel, and Iran.

2. Place a second transparency over the first and color in a second color the peoples that are of common, Semitic ethnicity. Semites are descendants of the Biblical Shem, referred to in the tenth chapter of Genesis. Countries that are generally Semitic would include all countries colored in #1 (above) plus Turkey and Israel. Most Iranians are Aryans who came there from regions to the East, such as Mongolia and China.

3. On a third transparency, color in a third color the countries in which most of the people follow the Muslim faith: the same countries of northern Africa, the Arabian peninsula, Turkey, Jordan, Syria, West Bank, the Gaza Strip, Lebanon, Iraq, and Iran. Mention to students that the Arab world extends east into Afghanistan and Pakistan. Note that you are omitting Israel.

4. On a fourth transparency, color in another color the major Middle East oil-producing countries: Saudi Arabia, Kuwait, Iraq, Iran, United Arab Emirates, Oman, and Syria.

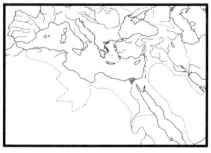

The Ottoman Empire

5. Explain that about 1300, before our country was settled by the Pilgrims, the Ottoman Empire in Turkey became very powerful, conquering much of the Middle East, northern Africa, and eastern Europe. The Ottoman Empire was largest about 1672, the same time as our Colonial Period. (Then it decreased in power until World War I when it lost much of its territory. In 1923 a republic was established.) On a fourth transparency, color in a fourth color the Ottoman Empire at its height: (If you are interested in the Ottoman Empire, Sultan Suleyman was an important and colorful ruler; check PBS for an excellent tape that is shown occasionally.) These countries have this historical background in common; they were conquered and controlled by others for hundreds of years.

6. Discuss with the class what all of this means. What do these

countries have in common? Did we color all the countries on every transparency? Why not? What other transparancies could we make?

7. Explain that the Middle East was originally called the Near East because for traders it was on the way from Europe to the Far East, India, and China. As traders passed through this region, they realized how important it was as a region itself, not just some land to pass through to reach somewhere else. We can see that a number of these countries are linked to one another in several ways. Remove all transparencies.

8. Replace all of the transparencies with a fifth one, a blank outline map. Use a dark marker.

    • Color in all of Africa. In our study of the Middle East we will not study about Africa, because the countries there do not have as much in common with the Middle East countries as the Middle East countries have with one another.
    • Color in Asia (Pakistan, Afghanistan, India, and the former U.S.S.R. to the dotted line above the Black Sea). We will not study Asia, for the same reasons.
    • Color in Europe (from the dotted line west). We will not study about Europe, for the same reasons. European countries have more in common with one another and are studied as a continent.
    • What is left is what we will study. (Point to the area left blank.) This, for our purposes, is the Middle East.
    • Display and distribute maps of the Middle East.

Part 2 Focussing on one country

1. Divide the class into cooperative learning groups.

2. Display the list of countries and guide each group to choose one to study.

3. Distribute maps to all group members for the countries they have chosen.

4. All groups have a time of free exploration in which they learn more about the country they chose. We strongly suggest you do not give a list of tasks, so that they can really "explore" the country and the areas around it. Here are some ways students can use a map:

    • Identify and label the country.
    • Locate the capital and other important cities.
    • Extend boundaries and identify neighboring countries.
    • Label distinctive geographical features.
    • Color countries and bodies of water appropriately.

Bahrain
Iran
Iraq
Israel
Occupied Territories:
    Golan Heights
    Gaza Strip
    West Bank
Jordan
Kuwait
Lebanon
Oman
Qatar
Saudi Arabia
Syria
Turkey
United Arab Emirates
Yemen

Part 3 Making posters (same groups)

1. Display the transparency of a resource sheet.

2. Read and discuss it together, identifying the most important information.

3. Discuss how some of this important information could be displayed on a map, flag or poster featuring that country [pictures of products, reports, etc.].

4. Distribute resource sheets on the assigned countries and poster materials to all groups.

5. Allow work time for constructing posters. Circulate to guide and help students to think why they decided various pieces of information were important.

6. Allow a separate time for groups to plan how they will present their posters to the whole class. A good procedure is to require that every student take part in the presentation.

Part 4 Sharing posters

1. Have groups give their presentations with their posters. It is important to be fair about time limits. Allow time *after all groups have presented* for class members to discuss information and ask questions.

TRY This

1. Now that students know how to judge their time, repeat the activity with other countries. Draw names to change the groupings.

2. Give extra credit for an individually made poster on any other Middle East country.

3. Make a videotaped "travel program" in which the posters are placed side-by-side and viewers are taken on a "tour" of them.

    • How are these countries similar?
    • How are they different?
    • What information was new to you?
    • Where could you find additional information about this country?

Bahrain

The State of Bahrain is a group of 33 islands midway between the peninsula of Qatar and the mainland of Saudi Arabia. Its total area is 265 square miles, about one-third the area of Rhode Island. When people refer to the country of Bahrain, they usually mean Bahrain Island, the largest island, from which the country gets its name. All but two of the other islands are uninhabited. Most of Bahrain Island is a flat and barren desert, but along the northern coast there is a wide fertile strip of land.

For a long time Bahrain has been a good place to work and live. Archeologists have found ancient grave mounds and temple ruins showing that people lived here many centuries ago. They hunted, farmed, fished, and even carried on trade with far away Mesopotamia. There Bahrain was described in ancient writings as a kind of paradise.

Bahrain has been famous for fishing, shipbuilding, trading, and—in the past— pearling. Boats are built according to designs used for centuries; the wood is brought from other countries such as India and Iraq. Several fishing methods are used, including arrow-shaped wooden traps laid along the shore so fish are trapped by the receding tides.

In recent years Bahrain has replaced Lebanon as the banking center of the Middle East. Many people also work in jobs related to oil; although some oil has been found there, most refineries process oil from Saudi Arabia. Currently plans are under way for building the largest aluminum refinery in the world. In northern Bahrain the people use irrigation to grow dates, almonds, pomegranates, bananas, and figs. Traditional crafts include pottery, weaving, basketwork, and embroidery.

In 1971 Bahrain became independent. It is ruled by an emir or sheik with a National Council. Arabic is the official language, although English is widely used in business. Islam is the state religion, and most of the people are Muslims.

This is one kind of boat used for fishing.

Iran

The Islamic Republic of Iran, a country slightly larger than Alaska, is located east of Iraq. There are mountains along the western border; these slope to a large, desert plateau. The narrow coastal plains bordering the Caspian Sea and the Persian Gulf provide land with some water for farming. Most of the people live in the north and northwest, where winters are cold and summers very warm. Rainfall averages about 10 inches a year for the whole country.

Tradition declares that women cover their faces in front of strangers.

For centuries Iran was called Persia. About half the people speak Persian or Farsi, the official language. It is written with Arabic characters, but the vocabulary is different, much like English and French using the same alphabet. Other languages spoken include Turkish, Kurdish, Arabic, and English. Islam is the official state religion, and most people are Muslims.

In the past, most of the people lived in rural areas as nomads, wandering about the deserts searching for pasture land for their sheep and horses. Since the discovery of oil, many have moved to the cities, hoping for a better life.

Mineral resources are oil, natural gas, coal, chromium, and copper. In the north and west, the people grow grains (wheat and barley), fruits (dates and grapes), vegetables, tea, and sugar beets. They raise sheep and cattle, too. On the the southern coast, the people grow citrus fruits and cotton.

Industries involve production of oil, cement, refined sugar, and textiles. The residue from refining sugar beets is used as livestock feed. Textiles include weaving cloth and carpets.

Iran has given us much in art, architecture, and literature. The most famous Iranian poet was Omar Khayyam, whose poem *The Rubaiyat* has been read by millions of people all over the world. Iranian builders discovered how to build round domes and various kinds of arches. Iranian artists and crafts workers are famous for their miniature paintings, ceramic tile mosaics, and handsome carpets.

In the traditional Iranian family, the father is in charge. Women have little freedom and few legal rights. During the 1950's and 1960's, the Shah of Iran granted women more rights and better education. In 1979, however, there was an Islamic Revolution and people were required to turn away from what were called the "ways of foreigners."

Iraq

The Republic of Iraq, a country slightly larger than Montana, is located northeast of Saudi Arabia. The country's major land feature is the river valley plain around the Tigris and Euphrates Rivers. This area was known in ancient times as Mesopotamia ("the land between two rivers"). There are also mountains in the north and deserts in the west and south.

The natural resources include oil, natural gas, phosphates, and sulfur. The people grow dates, wheat, barley, rice, cotton, sugar cane, tobacco, and citrus fruits. They raise poultry, sheep, goats, and cattle. Industries include oil refining, textiles, cement, and phosphates (used to make fertilizer).

The people are mostly Arabs, with some Kurds and Turks. The official language is Arabic, and almost all of the people are Muslims. Several ancient civilizations were located here, including Babylon, Ur, Baghdad, and Nineveh. We know about the life of these people because archeologists have found pottery, tools, and other articles they used. These civilizations are described in the Bible and in other ancient writings.

The Sumerians, the earliest known settlers of Mesopotamia, were the first people to use written language. They probably invented the wheel, one of the most important inventions of all time. They had a calendar based on the farming seasons, and they found ways to help people farm in one place instead of wandering as nomads. They established laws, government, and even taxes to pay for the services provided. People built houses with stone and sun-dried bricks, and worked as weavers, potters, and silversmiths, as well as in other crafts. They bartered (traded) what they made or grew for food or other needs. Soon after Baghdad, the capital, was founded in A.D. 762, it became a center of trade and Islamic art. Baghdad is located on the Tigris River, at the point where it is closest to the Euphrates.

In recent years, Iraq has fought with Iran. In August, 1990, Iraq invaded the neighboring country of Kuwait, starting an international crisis known in the United States as the Gulf War.

Sometimes people farm using oxen and hand plows.

Israel

The State of Israel is a relatively small, heavily populated country on the eastern shore of the Mediterranean Sea. Because of its location and fertility, this land has been conquered and claimed by many nations at various times in history. Israel has a fertile coastal plain. Inland in the north, there are mountains and another plain. The southern half of the country is desert, but recently there has been some farming there with irrigation.

Most people in Israel are Jewish, either orthodox, conservative, liberal, or non-observing. There are also Muslims and a few Christians; most of these are Arabs.

These are Israeli postage stamps.

In general, the weather is cool and rainy in winter and then hot in summer, much warmer during the day than at night. It is especially hot by the Dead Sea, while along the coast there is often a nice ocean breeze.

The capital city of Jerusalem is Israel's largest city, with a population of half a million. Here are located the Israeli president's residence, the parliament, the Supreme Court, and other government buildings. The Wailing Wall, part of the Second Temple, is a place where Jews from all over the world come to pray. Muslims believe that a nearby rock was the one on which Abraham was prepared to offer his son Isaac as a sacrifice; they built a gold-domed mosque, the Dome of the Rock, to mark the place. For Christians the holiest site is the Church of the Holy Sepulchre, which is believed to be the place where Jesus was buried and resurrected. Many tourists enjoy visiting Jerusalem and other places in Israel where events in the Bible took place.

Most of the people live in cities and towns, but some live in cooperative villages where people live, eat, and work together on farms and then share the profits; homes and land belong to the state. In a **kibbutz**, the people eat in large dining halls and the children may live together in children's homes. In a **moshav**, children live with their parents and each family has a home and a plot of land.

Israel's major mineral resources are potash, copper, and phosphates. Phosphate and potash are combined to make fertilizer. Lacking most basic raw materials, the people use technology and creativity to manufacture products with a high value. Industries include diamond cutting, food processing, tourism, textiles, electronics, and manufacturing machinery. The people grow citrus fruits and vegetables, and raise cattle and sheep. There is also some fishing along the coast.

The Occupied Territories

In the War of 1967, Israel captured and occupied the Golan Heights, West Bank, and the Gaza Strip. The U.N. said Israel could not keep these territories they had won by war but agreed Israel should keep order in them.

Before 1967, West Bank had been part of Jordan, or Transjordan as it was then called. The land is hilly, with a narrow valley on the east. In general, the weather is cool and rainy in winter and then hot in summer. It is especially hot in the Jordan Valley and along the Dead Sea, with a great difference between day and night temperatures.

Most of the Israelis here work in Jerusalem. Many Palestinians have also done this until recently, when Israeli authorities prohibited Palestinian Arabs from crossing the border. Other Palestinians run small businesses, farm small pieces of land, and raise flocks of sheep or goats on the barren land. There are schools and several Palestinian universities in West Bank.

The Gaza Strip is a narrow piece of land along the Mediterranean Sea. Inland the fertile coastal plain quickly changes to desert. Most of the Palestinians here live along the coast in refugee camps, many without running water or electricity. Some farm or run small businesses, but most have had jobs in Israel.

Before 1967, the Golan Heights had been part of Syria. Because of the cliffs here (overlooking Israeli land), Israelis felt unsafe. In 1981, as a result, Israel formally annexed the Golan Heights and declared them part of Israel.

The Palestinian Arabs in all three territories live in villages and large refugee camps. In recent years, hundreds of

Courtesy of Aramco World

"Want to buy some flowers?"

Israelis have built homes here. The Palestinians object, claiming the land on which they build has belonged to Palestinian families for many years.

Since 1948, when Israel was established, there has been trouble in the occupied territories between the Israelis and the Palestinians. Finally, in September, 1993, the President of Israel and the Chairman of the PLO (Palestine Liberation Organization) signed an agreement to begin the peace process. Although there are still problems, many hope that peace is coming.

Jordan

The Hashemite Kingdom of Jordan, east of Israel, is about the same size as Kentucky. The Jordan River divides the country into two parts, the East Bank and the West Bank. Since the War of 1967, Israel has occupied the West Bank. Most of the rest of Jordan is barren desert with a few oases.

Along the Jordan River and the Dead Sea is a narrow strip of fertile land, the lowest land on earth. Here the people produce crops in a climate that is warm throughout the year. At the southern extreme of the country is Aqaba, Jordan's only seaport. East of this valley are the highlands. Here the weather is generally wet and cool. This is where most of the people live. The rest of Jordan is a semi-arid desert, with enough rainfall in spring and fall that small plants grow for flocks to graze. Temperature varies a lot from day to night; summers are generally hot and dry, while winters are cold and windy.

The main mineral resources are phosphate and potash, which are combined to make fertilizer. The people grow grains (wheat, barley, lentils), olives, vegetables (tomatoes, eggplant), and fruits (oranges, grapes, figs). The nomad herders raise sheep, goats, horses, and camels. (Horses are not used for food.) They import much of their meat and wheat. because they cannot grow enough.

Most of the people of Jordan are Arabs, either Bedouins or Palestinians. Bedouins are the original nomad settlers, while Palestinians are immigrants who lost their homes and land when Israel was established or during the Arab-Israeli wars of 1967 and 1973. Most of the people are Muslims. Arabic is the official language, although many Jordanians also speak English. Most people can read and write. Many people live in small villages in flat-roofed houses built of stone or sun-dried brick.One interesting feature of Jordan is Petra, an ancient city in which the rose-colored buildings were carved into great sandstone cliffs many centuries ago. It is considered an architectural masterpiece.

Photo courtesy of Aramco World

An Arab teacher challenges his students.

Kuwait

The State of Kuwait, a country slightly larger than Hawaii, is located at the northeast corner of the Arabian peninsula. Most of it is a flat and sandy desert, with little rain, no rivers, and no lakes. The weather is hot and dry.

Most of the original settlers came to what was then a small coastal town, leaving the desert to find a better life. People earned their living fishing, pearling, and building boats. Kuwaiti seamen were well known throughout that part of the world. Some people were nomads, who wandered the deserts, herding animals and searching for grazing lands. Kuwait became an important seaport in the area

Through the years the Kuwaitis have asked for protection from the British. In 1961 this protection was withdrawn and Kuwait became an independent country. In 1990 Iraq invaded Kuwait and the United States sent troops to help drive the invaders out. This was known as the Gulf War.

Since oil was first exported from Kuwait in 1946, people have come from a wider area, including Europe, to work in the oil industry. More than half of the people now living there came from some other country. Other industries, much less important, include making chemical fertilizers, sand-and-lime brick, concrete, and tile. Diving for pearls used to be a profitable industry. However, since the Japanese found a way to grow—or "culture"—pearls at a much lower cost, people have not wanted to pay the higher prices for pearls obtained by diving.

Arabic is the official language, although English is also spoken there. Islam is the official religion. The country is wealthy because of the oil production. As a result, every person who lives there receives free education, medical care, and social security.

Because there is not enough rain for farming, even with irrigation, agriculture is limited. As a result, most food is imported from other countries.

Refineries of various kinds are an important part of the landscape in the Middle East.

Lebanon

The Republic of Lebanon is north of Israel on the Mediterranean Sea, with an area smaller than Connecticut. East of the coastal plain are the Lebanon and Anti-Lebanon Mountains, with the fertile Bekaa Valley between them. A river runs from north to south through the valley, then turns west to empty into the Mediterranean.

The weather is rainy and mild in winter and then hot in summer. The snow and rain that falls in the mountains drains down into the Bekaa Valley and the coastal plain. Lebanon has no deserts.

When the country gained its independence in 1946, the Muslims, Christians, and Druze formed political groups and fought for power. Many people have been killed and much property destroyed as the various groups have fought among themselves and with Israel. In 1990, peace was restored, but the country has been hurt. Tourists and business people have not wanted to go there because they have not felt safe.

Lebanon's resources are limited to farmland and small amounts of limestone, iron, and a few other minerals. Much of the country's past prosperity has been commerce and tourism because of its location and seaports. There were trading, ship building, tourism, and other related businesses.

Since the cities and the southern part of the country have been troubled, farming (in the north and in the Bekaa Valley) has become even more important. They raise grains, vegetables, fruits, and poultry. On the coastal plain they grow oranges, lemons, bananas, almonds, and dates. On the hillsides there are olive and fig trees, grape vines, and cattle grazing.

Because of Lebanon's commercial and cultural history, there are festivals and ancient ruins that people from all over the world have enjoyed visiting in the past. The Cedars of Lebanon, beautiful groves of cedar trees, are world famous, as is the hospitality of the people. Many hope that someday soon, Lebanon will return to its place in the world.

In Lebanon the people grow fruits, especially in the Bekaa Valley

Oman

The Sultanate of Oman is located on the southeast coast of the Arabian peninsula, bordering on the Gulf of Oman and the Arabian Sea. It is about the size of Utah and has a coastline of nearly a thousand miles. There are coastal plains which rise into barren mountains in the north and south. The rest of the land is stony desert. A small area belonging to Oman is located at the tip of the peninsula to the north, controlling entrance to the Persian Gulf. Some of the hottest temperatures in the world are recorded in Oman, and there is little rainfall.

Most Omanis are Arabs, with some non-Arabs living in the coastal cities. Arabic is the official language, but English, Urdu, and other languages are also spoken. Almost all of the people are Muslim, although some who settled here are from India. The country is ruled by a sultan, which is why it is called a sultanate.

Long ago, the people here lived quietly: farming, fishing, or herding flocks. Along the coast they raised dates, coconuts, fruits, and grains. The nomad shepherds raised goats and camels. In the 1960's, oil was discovered. Although many of the people still work in fishing and farming, the country's income is now mainly from the sale of crude oil to other countries. Although the country has a lot more money than before, there are many needs, such as in health and education.

In addition to the oil there, Oman's natural resources include copper, asbestos, marble, and limestone. In addition to selling crude oil to other countries, they produce cement. There has been much more construction in Oman since oil was discovered.

Oman is interesting because much of it is old and unchanged. Some of its cities were famous in the ancient world, although they were known by different names. In modern times, the discovery of oil has brought about some changes, and Oman has gained world importance.

Scenes like this were common long ago.

Qatar

The State of Qatar is located on the Persian Gulf coast of the Arabian Peninsula. It is smaller than Connecticut. The land is flat and barren, with some limestone ridges. The weather is hot, and most of the country is very dry. Along the coast, where there is a small amount of rain, the people do some farming. Most of the people live on the east coast, around Doha, the capital and center of business.

Of all the people that live in Qatar, only one-fourth were born there. The rest have come to work in the oil industry. Half of the people come from other Arab countries.

Arabic is the most widely spoken language, but English, Persian, and Urdu are also spoken. Most people follow the Islamic faith, and some are Hindus. The country has been independent since 1971, ruled by a sheikh and an advisory council.

Qatar is a good example of a poor country that became rich when oil was discovered. While oil production and refining are the major industries, the country has used some of the income from it to develop commercial fishing and to improve farming methods. They grow wheat and vegetables; they now grow enough tomatoes that they can export some. Other industries include natural gas development and cement production.

Through the years, Qatar has been ruled by many other countries, including Bahrain, Turkey, and Great Britain. With British help the people have made many improvements, such as developing the harbor and airport at Doha, building steel and cement plants, and constructing a road to Saudi Arabia.

In Qatar there is a national museum with interesting objects related to the history of the area. There is also a library with over a thousand ancient Arabic manuscripts and many prehistoric objects.

Photo courtesy of Aramco World

How many gallons of oil do you think this huge tanker holds?

Saudi Arabia

The Kingdom of Saudi Arabia occupies most of the Arabian Peninsula. It is about one-third the size of the United States. On the west, all along the Red Sea, is a narrow plain and then high, barren mountains. From there, the land slopes toward the Persian Gulf. There is very little rainfall, except along the coast and in the capital city of Riyadh, which is built in a large oasis. There are no rivers or permanent bodies of water.

Photo courtesy of Aramco World
Soccer is very popular here.

Saudi Arabia's major resource is oil. They sell more oil to other countries than any other nation in the world. Many people who used to be nomadic herders of sheep, goats, and camels now live in the cities and have jobs related to the oil industry. Although there is very little rainfall, the people have used the income from oil to irrigate desert land to grow dates, barley, wheat, and some fruit.

Most of the people are Arabs, although many foreigners, Arabs and non-Arabs, come for limited periods of time to work in the oil refineries and related businesses. Arabic is the official language. Islam is the official religion, and the country uses the Koran, the sacred book of Islam, as the system of laws. Most people speak Arabic, although English is also spoken in the cities.

Mecca and Medina, two cities in Saudi Arabia, are important to Muslims throughout the world. All faithful Muslims try to make a pilgrimage to Mecca, the birthplace of Mohammed (Islam's founder) at least once in their lives.

Medina is significant because the tomb of Mohammed is located there in the beautiful Mosque of the Prophet.

Since the 1930's, the country has been ruled by a king with a council of ministers. Although there is no voting in Saudi Arabia, the king and other officials have weekly sessions in which all citizens can express their opinions and make requests.

Syria

The Syrian Arab Republic is about the size of Missouri. It is located east of Lebanon and Israel, with a small strip of land on the Mediterranean Sea coast. There are north-to-south mountains. Then the country slopes east and south toward the Euphrates River. In the south are rather barren areas of mountains, plateaus, and deserts. The Golan Heights, an area in the southwest, was captured by Israel in the 1967 war and formally annexed by Israel in 1981.

Many Syrians are Arabs, with the rest mostly Kurds and Armenians. Nearly everyone speaks Arabic, either as a first or a second language. English, French, Kurdish, and Armenian are also spoken. Most Syrians are Muslims. Although there are fewer Christians than Muslims, more of the Christians have learned to speak English and other foreign languages. As a result, they have been able to associate with European and American businesses and governments. This has led to some difficulties between the Muslims and the Christians.

The country's major mineral resources are crude oil, phosphates, chrome, and iron. Industries are oil refining, textiles, glassware, and cement. They grow cotton, grains, olives, fruits, and vegetables. Sugar beets are grown and refined here. They raise sheep and goats. Some people still live in villages of small, flat-topped houses, while others live in more modern apartment buildings. Many places in Syria are mentioned in the Bible, although they may be called by different names.

Syrians have been famous for their poetry. Long ago, Syrian poets would read their poetry to large crowds of people.

This girl is Syrian. Does she look like anyone you know?

Turkey

The Republic of Turkey is located between the Mediterranean Sea and the Black Sea. It is twice the size of California. Although most of Turkey is in Asia, a small piece is in Europe. Turkey is often called the *Gateway to the Middle East* . It has a very long coastline, with fertile plains and many prosperous seaports. Inland there are mountains surrounding a high and somewhat barren plateau that is cold in winter and hot in summer.

Major mineral resources include chromium, copper, and other minerals, but much of this has not been developed. A mineral called meerschaum is made into world-famous tobacco pipes. Wood from the forests is another important resource. The people have vineyards and groves of olive trees. They raise cattle, sheep, and goats for food, wool, and leather. (Mohair comes from goats in Angora.) In the southern and western coastal plains, the people raise cotton, wheat, citrus fruits, grapes, and figs. The northern coast is more industrial, but they also grow tea, hazelnuts, and the famous Turkish tobacco there. Industries include textiles, mining, steel production, and oil refining. Turkish carpets are world-famous. Turkish coffee is really a method of brewing coffee, rather than a type of coffee grown in Turkey.

The people are mostly Turks, with some Kurds and Armenians. Most of the people speak Turkish, but Kurdish and Arabic are also spoken. Nearly all of the people are Muslims. Half of the people live in small farm villages, in houses made of stone or sun-dried brick; the other half live in cities like Istanbul and Ankara.

Turkish people enjoy gathering to talk or to celebrate special occasions. Big cities have parks (much like our own) and also "tea gardens" where families can go to have fun. There is play equipment and usually a stand where they can buy sandwiches and other snacks. Smaller towns have at least one coffee house. Here the men gather to watch television, exchange farming news, talk politics, or play backgammon. Throughout Turkey the boys and men enjoy wrestling and soccer, which is called futbol there.

A number of places in the Bible are located in the area that is now the country of Turkey. Ephesus, Galatia, and Colossae are all ancient names for some of the cities in Turkey. Many tourists enjoy visiting these historical sites.

Photo courtesy of Aramco World

School's out!

United Arab Emirates

The United Arab Emirates (U. A. E.) is located on the Persian Gulf. Its area is about the same as that of South Carolina. In the south and west there are mostly sand dunes and salt flats,with a few oases where palm trees and some vegetables grow. In the north and east there are stony plains and mountains. Along the northern and eastern coasts there are fertile plains where some crops are grown.

One-third of the people are Arabs, the rest foreigners who have come to work in the oil industry. There are very few nomads. Most people live along the coast, where the weather is hot and humid in summer and cool and rainy in winter.

The U. A. E. is a collection of seven small emirates, each ruled by an emir or sheik. Years ago, the area was called the Pirate Coast because pirates would rob ships (mostly British) and hide in the many inlets along the coast. In 1820, Great Britain agreed to protect these emirates if they would outlaw piracy and slave trade. In 1971 the emirates were united in one independent country.

People have lived in this area for thousands of years. Very old flint tools can still be found in the deserts and lower mountains. Tourists and residents enjoy visiting the ancient forts, tombs, settlements, and mosques. Ancient writings tell of much fishing and pearling. Fishing is still done, but since oil was discovered, the petroleum industry is what has given the country its great wealth. The government has used the money from oil to develop new ways of farming and saving water. They even remove the salt from ocean water. The people grow enough poultry and vegetables to feed the country most of the year. Alfalfa and grain crops are raised to feed the cattle and poultry.

Camels used to be very important as beasts of burden, also providing meat, milk, and leather. Now, the people do not depend on them as much, because they use cars and buy meat from other countries. A few camels are kept for meat, milk, and the popular camel races.

Photo courtesy of Aramco World
From the control tower this man supervises movements in a port.

Yemen

The Republic of Yemen is located on the southern coast of the Arabian Peninsula, in an area larger than Montana. The coast is sandy with volcanic rock; inland there are mountains and high plateaus. In the southern highlands there is some rainfall; the rain flows down from the highlands in wadis or riverbeds that are dry much of the year. Water, collected in wells, is used for watering crops. Toward the northeast part of the country, the highlands level off into desert.

Resources include crude oil, rock salt, coal, and copper. Industries are food processing, mining, and petroleum refining. The people grow small amounts of wheat, sorghum, fruits, coffee, and cotton. They raise sheep and do some commercial fishing. Most of the people work in farming or fishing, but most of the country's income is from oil.

In ancient times, Yemen was part of the kingdom of Saba or Sheba. There was much trade with ports of Africa and India. The Bible mentions the Queen of Sheba taking gifts of gold, spices, and precious stones to King Solomon in Jerusalem.

Yemen is made up of two countries, North Yemen (Yemen Arab Republic) and South Yemen (People's Democratic Republic of Yemen). In 1990 they agreed to unite. Most of the people are Arabic; they speak Arabic and follow the Islamic faith. Few of the people can read or write, although this situation is improving.

Since the coastal port of Aden is in a strategic location at the entrance to the Red Sea, it has long been a center for business and industry as well as a naval base. It has become even busier as a refueling stop since the Suez Canal was opened in 1869. In Aden there is a good standard of living with good schools and hospitals, but elsewhere in the country people are not as fortunate. In the highlands, the few people that live there farm the land or raise animals. Not many people live in the desert, because of the lack of water for crops or animals.

This type of fishing boat is called a dhu.

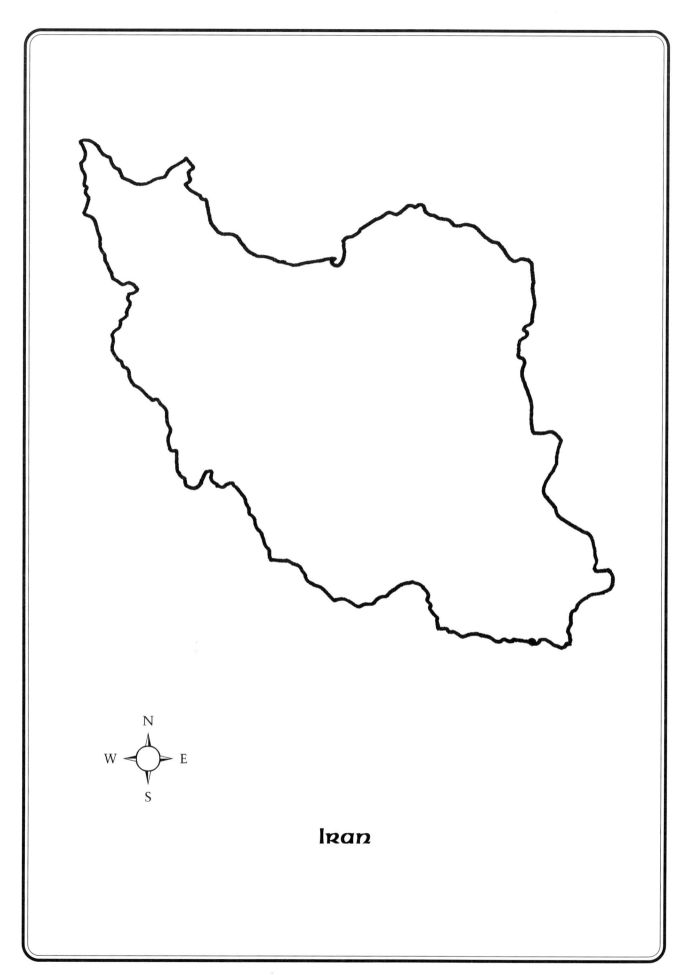

Iran

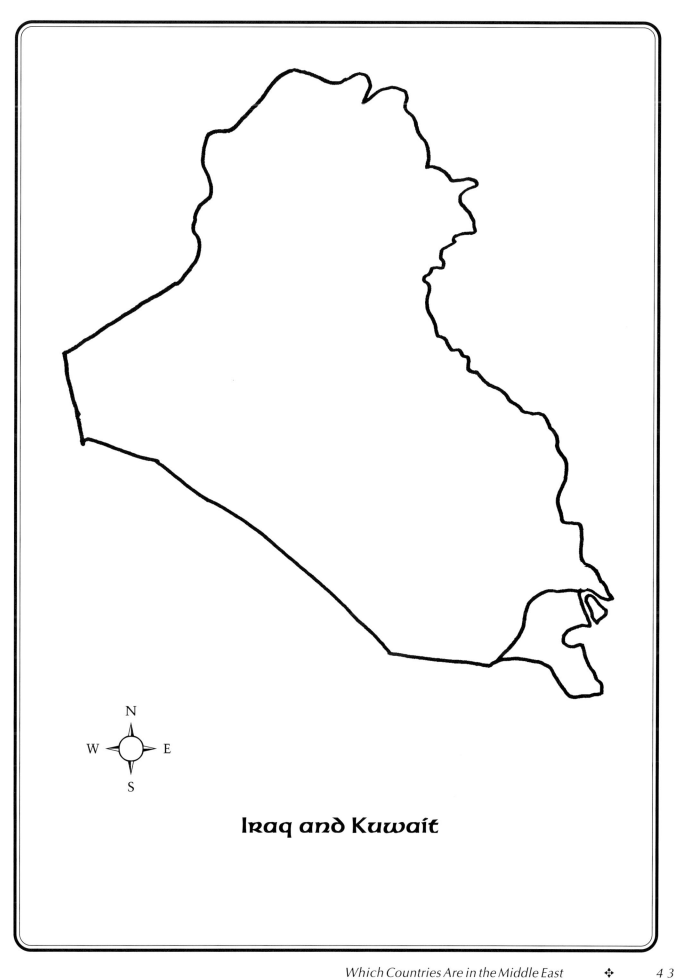

Iraq and Kuwait

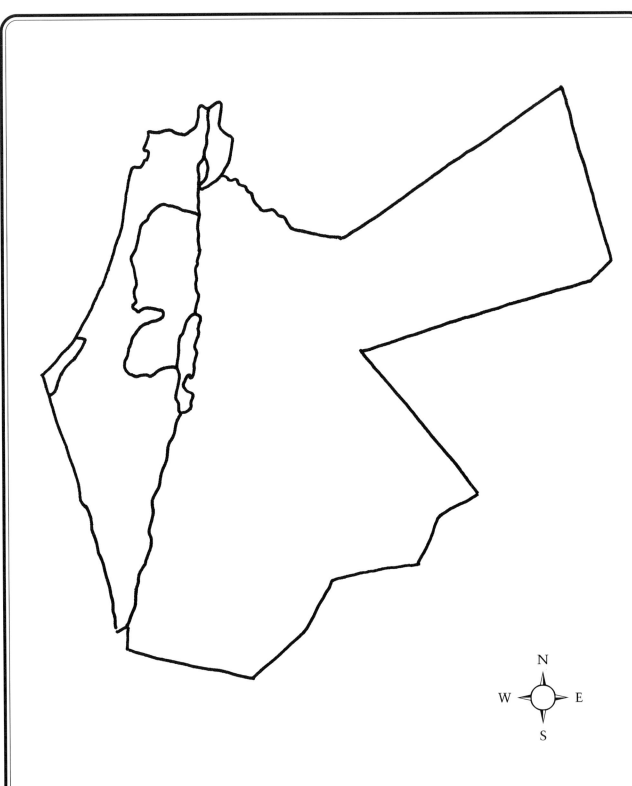

Jordan, Israel, and Occupied Territories

- · Gaza Strip
- · Golan Heights
- · West Bank

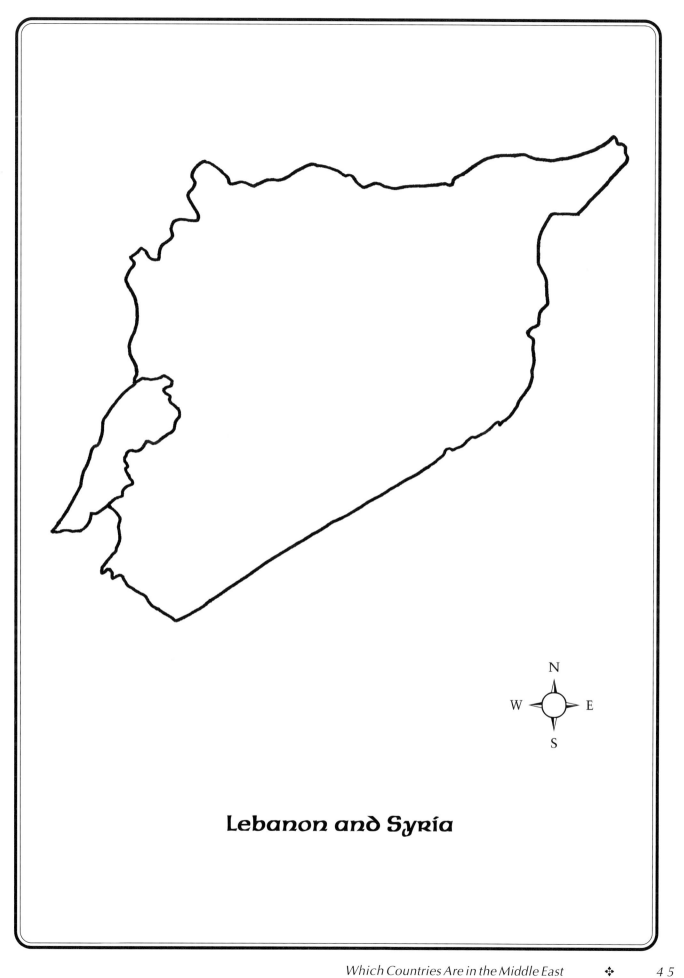

Lebanon and Syria

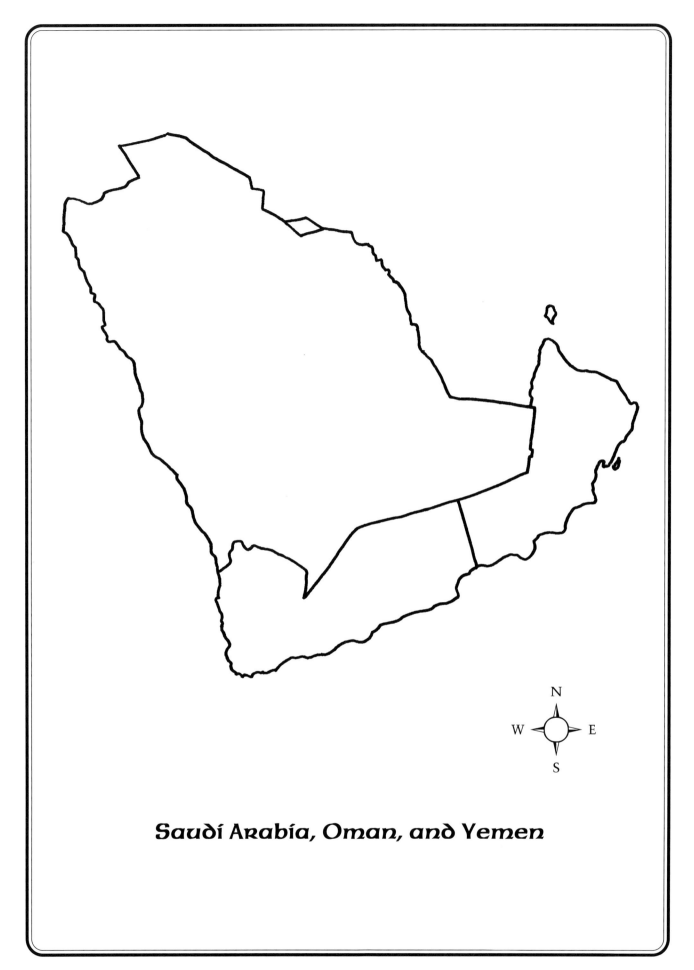

Saudi Arabia, Oman, and Yemen

Turkey

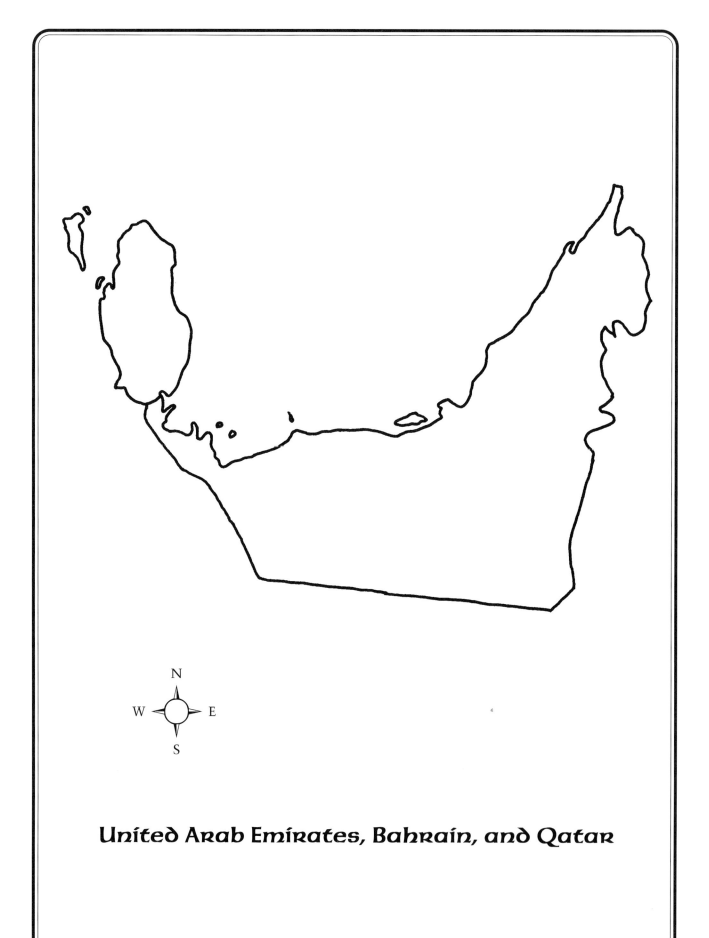

United Arab Emirates, Bahrain, and Qatar

6   Square Miles and Money

Focus

Students will compare countries using as measures the number of people per square mile and per capita income.

Resources

World map
Current world almanac
Optional: other reference books such as encyclopedias

Background

It is useful to compare countries by computing the number of people per square mile (PPSM) for each one. Since a higher PPSM means more people, one question would be how they are distributed. Another would be what skills they have, how they can contribute to the country's economy.

Another dimension is a country's Gross National Product (GNP). This is the total amount of money (real or theoretical) that a country receives for all of the goods and services it produces in a given year. In this activity, the GNP is divided by the population to give per capita (per person) income (PCI). For convenience, it is stated in U. S. dollars. There are many questions the PCI does not answer. Is there a large average group, for example, or, instead, a society of very rich and very poor?

Teaching Tips

1. The purpose of this activity is to increase the number of angles from which a student views a country, giving a deeper understanding. For this reason, we have included some additional information about each country, the capital and the monetary unit. Use these with the extensions to expand still further the students' knowledge base.

2. Beforehand, decide how you will use the activity sheets. We suggest dividing the class into cooperative learning groups and having each group choose a country to study. Decide

what information you want students to have at the beginning of the lesson and fill it in before making copies.

3. Beforehand, decide whether or not you want students to use calculators in coumputing the PPSM figures.

4. A current world almanac will provide the statistical information for identifying non-Middle East countries with similar PPSM's. Be sure students choose familiar countries for comparison, so that this part of the activity makes the statistics more meaningful.

Procedure

Part 1

1. Check that students can pronounce the names of the countries and capitals.

2. Test students' skills in reading large numbers. Encourage them to read the numbers orally throughout the activity when discussing them.

3. Use a world map to make some calculations about the sizes of the various countries in the Middle East. Explain that today we are going to compare countries by finding out how many people are in a square mile, on average. Discuss PPSM and the concept of *average.*

4. Find the PPSM for each country by dividing the total population by the area.

5. List countries on the chalkboard according to their PPSM, from highest to lowest. (Leave room for a comparative list of the countries according to individual incomes found in *Part 2.*) Discuss the implications, in view of what students already know about Middle East countries.

Part 2

1. Discuss the meaning of GNP. Then find the per capital income (PCI) by dividing the GNP of each country by its population.

2. Make a second list of countries according to their PCI's. Save the last column to record the PCI's of other countries.

3. Help students to identify the standings of various countries in the two lists.

- What does this tell us about the wealth and area of these countries?
- What does a country need to be prosperous?
- How does this information confirm or deny your impression of these countries?

Try This

1. Find out the PPSM and PCI of the United States and compare them with countries in the Middle East. What is surprising?

2. Make a bulletin board of a world map. Connect with one color yarn the pairs of countries identified as having a similar PPSM, with a different color for income per person. Be sure to allow time for students to examine the map and discuss these pairings.

3. Calculate the GNP of a country in terms of <u>its</u> local monetary unit. Find approximate exchange rates in the almanac or more accurately in the *Wall Street Journal*. (Consult a local bank for countries not listed.)

4. Use the *World Almanac* to compare the U.S. budget (total) with that of various Middle East countries. Do any countries have budgets larger than that of the United States?

Square Miles and Money - Part 1

Which of these countries has the most people per square mile or PPSM?
How can you find out?

Country or Territory	Capital	Total Population	Area (sq. mi.)	People Per Square Mile (PPSM)
Bahrain	Manama	500,000	300	
Iran	Teheran	60,000,000	600,000	
Iraq	Baghdad	20,000,000	200,000	
Israel	Jerusalem	4,000,000	8,000	
Occupied Territories	none	not available	not available	
Jordan	Amman	3,500,000	200,000	
Kuwait	Kuwait City	2,300,000	7,000	
Lebanon	Beirut	3,400,000	4,000	
Oman	Muscat	1,600,000	80,000	
Qatar	Doha	500,000	4,000	
Saudi Arabia	Riyadh	17,000,000	800,000	
Syria	Damascus	13,200,000	70,000	
Turkey	Ankara	59,000,000	300,000	
United Arab Emirates	Abu Dhabi	2,500,000	30,000	
Yemen	Sana	12,000,000	200,000	

What does this tell you about these countries?

Square Miles and Money - Part 2

Country or Territory	Monetary Unit	Total Population	Gross Nat'l Product(GNP)	Per Capita Income (PCI)	Country With Similar PCI
Bahrain	Bahraini dinar	500,000	300		
Iran	rial	60,000,000	600,000		
Iraq	Iraqi dinar	20,000,000	200,000		
Israel	shekel	4,000,000	8,000		
Occupied Territories	shekel	1,800,000	3,000		
Jordan	Jordanian dinar	3,500,000	200,000		
Kuwait	Kuwaiti dinar	2,300,000	7,000		
Lebanon	Lebanese pound	3,400,000	4,000		
Oman	Omani riyal	1,600,000	80,000		
Qatar	Qatari riyal	500,000	4,000		
Saudi Arabia	Saudi riyal	17,000,000	800,000		
Syria	Syrian pound	13,200,000	70,000		
Turkey	Turkish lira	59,000,000	300,000		
United Arab Emirates	dirham	2,500,000	30,000		
Yemen	Yemeni rial	12,000,000	200,000		

What does the PCI tell you?

(GNP from U.N. and accurate as of January, 1992.)

7   Trade!

Focus

Students learn about the resources of the Middle East by playing a trading-type card game.

Resources

resource game cards provided (see *Teaching Tips*)

Background

The term "resource" is customarily used to refer to goods and services which can be sold for revenue. For many centuries farmland was considered the major resource of a country; the amount of farmland would determine how many people could be fed. As transportation improved, a broader idea of resource developed, because food (and other goods) could be bought and sold on a broader market. However, the land had to be used for crops for which there was a demand, and the crops had to be sold at an appropriate market price.

Many countries in the Middle East have been considered low in resources because geographically they have not had farmland which would allow them to support large populations and participate in the world market. It had been known for centuries that there was oil in the Middle East, but the world market did not have a high demand for oil until the invention of the automobile. Accompanying the mass production of Fords there was a sudden rise in demand for petroleum products. The oil supply had been there all the time, but now there was a demand. Parts of the Middle East became wealthy overnight, changing the economics and history of the area—and the world.

A closer look at the definition of a resource reveals that the *services* portion includes people and their ingenuity. For example, a region like the San Joaquin Valley in California is really desert, much poorer land than the fertile plains of the midwestern United States. However, enterprising farmers have found ways to irrigate and fertilize the land, transforming it into a magnificent resource that feeds much of the world. Similarly the tourist industry has capitalized upon the beauty of some areas which do not have agricultural or mining natural resources. The Industrial Revolution carried this still farther, making it possible for an area lacking agricultural resources to produce wealth and support a large number of people. The management of resources has always been an important issue. In modern times a discussion of resources often focuses upon the use of non-renewable natural resources to produce wealth some do not feel we really need. For example, have we become so extravagant in our use of oil that we ignore the air and land pollution which this produces? This activity provides an opportunity to discuss such issues and raise students' awareness. If all you do is play the game, you are missing the point.

See also *Resources of the Middle East -Resource Sheet*

Teaching Tips

1. Divide into groups of 4-6 players.

2. Prepare 6 copies of the resource game cards for each group. Copy cards on tagboard or glue paper copies on 3" by 5" cards. Laminate if desired.

Procedure

1. Before or after playing the game, discuss what resources are and specifically what the resources of your own community are. Find out what they know about the resources of the Middle East, and use *Resources of the Middle East - Resource Sheet* (or other references) to enhance the discussion.

2. To play the game, the dealer in each group shuffles the cards and distributes 6 cards to each player, with the remainder (the *surplus commodity storage*) placed in the middle of the table.

3. The dealer asks any player for a card matching one in dealer's hand. If that player holds such a card, it must be given to the dealer. If not, that player says "Go trade!" and the dealer draws one from the surplus commodity storage. Play passes to the left of the dealer.

4. Play continues until one player has collected a *complete set*, 6 copies of any one commodity. This is the end of a round. If a player has no cards, he or she may draw one from the surplus commodity storage, to be used the following turn. Play as many rounds as time allows.

Try This

1. Play the game in pairs to promote cooperation or to include students unable to play without help.

2. Have students make a *Trade!* game for a specific Middle East country. Research the resources that are appropriate, design the cards, and decide on the rules to be followed.

3. Write short reports on the products, using the *Pyramid Method* (see the *Skills and Strategies* chapter.)

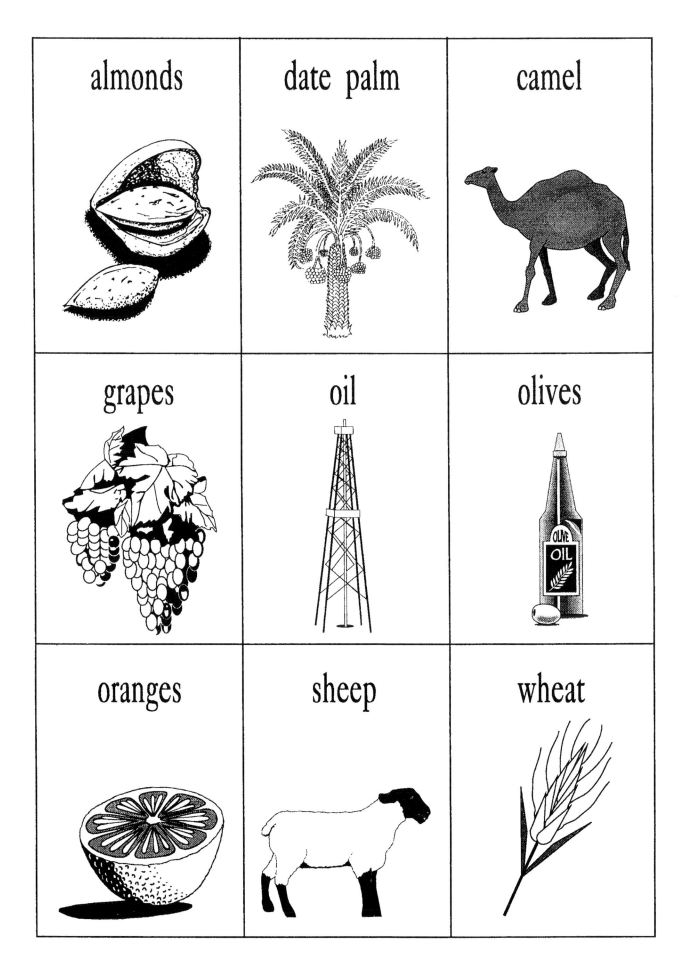

almonds

date palm

camel

grapes

oil

olives

oranges

sheep

wheat

Resources of the Middle East

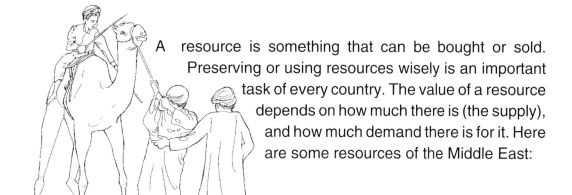

A resource is something that can be bought or sold. Preserving or using resources wisely is an important task of every country. The value of a resource depends on how much there is (the supply), and how much demand there is for it. Here are some resources of the Middle East:

Camels: They drink up to 50 gallons of water in a few hours, eat almost anything (including cacti), and can move at fourteen miles an hour. Use of trucks and paved roads have cut the demand for camels for transporting goods.

Dates and Grapes: These fruits have been popular because they can be eaten fresh or dried without refrigeration. Date palm trees and grapevines do not need much water. Date pits (seeds) are ground up for animal feed.

Wheat: Grains such as wheat, barley, rice, and alfalfa were probably cultivated first in the Middle East. They are used in stews, soups, and salads. Wheat is ground into flour for pita bread.

Sheep: In the Middle East, the people can raise sheep, goats, and cattle on land where soil is too poor to raise crops.

Oil: Although people knew about oil long ago, it has become important in modern times because of automobiles. About half of the world's petroleum (unrefined oil) comes from the Middle East.

Almonds: These and other tasty nuts are native to the Middle East and originally grew wild there. They have been a food source for thousands of years.

Oranges: Citrus fruits were first grown in the Middle East many years ago. The bright sunshine of the Middle East is just what citrus trees need.

Olives: Olive trees grow slowly on little water and live for hundreds of years. Olives are pickled or pressed for their oil. The leaves are considered symbols of peace.

8   Don't Cry Over Spilled Oil

Focus

Students will learn about the pollution of oil spills by trying to remove oil from water, sand, and plants.

Resources

For the whole class:
clipping of an oil spill (as recent as possible)

For each group:

small (pot-pie type) aluminum foil pans
small amounts of natural materials:
    sand, rocks, small plants, feathers, and so on
variety of clean-up materials:
    cotton balls, string, yarn, liquid detergent,
    styrofoam pellets, sponge, paper towels,
    and so on

2 Tbsp. <u>used</u> motor or gear oil
liquid detergent
spoons
sheet plastic or newspaper to protect tables
half-gallon milk carton for disposing of used
    materials
clock with second hand (can be class wall clock)

Background

Oil spills from off-shore wells and giant tankers affect thousands of marine plants and animals and their food chains. Scientists do not know the long-term effects of oil spills.

One example of a bird suffering the effect of oil spills is a rare species called Socutra Comorants. According to the Saudi Meteorological and Environmental Protection Agency, one spill may have killed as many as 14,000 of these, with less than one-tenth of the oiled birds making their way to the Saudi bird hospital. In such cases, the birds must be kept warm until they are healthy enough to be washed. Cleaning each one may take up to 25 gallons of water (kept at temperatures between 102 and 110 degrees Fahrenheit) and using up to two hours of labor. One difficulty is the birds' beaks; they must be taped shut to prevent them from pecking the workers. In confusion, the birds often drown from diving into the soapy, oily water. Another difficulty is the presence of solvents in the oil; these destroy the natural oil on the birds' feathers, preventing them from floating.

Understanding the characteristics of oil itself is important. For example, it floats on water. This means it will spread into huge slicks on the ocean and cover anything it touches. Methods used for cleaning up oil spills may take advantage of this attribute by (1) placing floating barriers or booms around the spill to limit its spread or (2) adding detergents to the oil so that it sinks. The latter strategy is controversial because of the way it may harm bottom-feeding marine life. In this activity, students are asked to predict whether the oil will float or sink, so that the teacher can judge whether or not this concept needs to be taught.

Few deny the problems connected with the transport and storage of oil. Some studies seem to show there is little permanent damage from oil spills, but many are skeptical of such studies and object to the high-level usage and waste of oil throughout the world. Most people agree that consumers of all ages need to raise their awareness regarding our oil-dependent lifestyles.

Teaching Tips

1. Use cooperative learning groups, assigning duties for the facilitator, the timer, the reporter, and the encourager. (See chapter on *Skills and Strategies* for help.).

2. Decide how to manage the materials. Will all students test the same materials?

3. Decide how much guidance you will give students in using various materials and methods. For example, the spoons could be used to scoop up the oil itself or the materials covered with oil; the detergent could be used diluted or undiluted, and so on.

Procedure

1. Discuss oil spills with the whole class enough to find out how much the students already know. Share the clipping.

2. Divide into groups. Cover the bottom of the aluminum pie pan with a layer of soil and rocks, and then make it higher on one side to form a "beach." Press in the small plants and feathers; remind students that the feathers show what happens to birds and animals which might be involved in an oil spill. Add enough water to make the water level about half way up the beach.

3. Distribute student record sheets and have groups make their predictions. **Be sure they explain the reasons for their predictions; this is one of the most valuable parts of the activity.**

4. Put the oil on the water. Let it spread, especially onto the beach, plants, and other materials placed there. Rock the container to simulate waves and tides.

5. In each group, decide who will test each material. Have the timer (person) say when to begin the one-minute test of each material. Students try to clean up as much oil as possible in the minute. As each material is tested, the recorder notes what happens. The manager decides when the next person begins testing another material.

6. When each group has finished testing all materials, they decide together which material seems to have done the best job. Be sure they record this.

7. As a class, have all groups share their test results. List for the class the materials various groups thought worked best. Test these again together to see which of them seems to be the best of all. Be sure to emphasize that these are <u>our</u> findings based on <u>our</u> tests; conclusions are tentative.

8. Discuss how easy or difficult it was to remove oil.

   • Does oil mix with water? How can you prove this?
   • Is oil that spills like this or is it clean like salad oil? [like this, not clean]
   • What other problems are caused by oil spills? [other plants, animals, etc.]
   • Why do people use a lot of oil? How could we change the way we live to use less oil? [Be specific in mentioning appliances and consumables common to your students' lifestyle: automobile usage, plastics of all kinds, etc.]
   • If we used less oil, would this mean fewer oil spills? Why?

Try This

1. Write a newspaper article explaining your clean-up effort and what you discovered.

2. Divide into two groups, the oil companies and the oil users. Carry on a conversation between two persons, one from each group, although others may coach. Discuss the advantages and risks of having societies in which oil plays such an important role. Include what impact oil spills have on life in the future.

3. Write a letter to your congressmen asking what the United States is doing to help clean up oil spills, and what precautions they believe should be taken to avoid these disasters.

4. Design a tool to remove oil from water using what you learned in the activity.

5. List vehicles and other machines that use sizable amounts of petroleum products. Be sure to include boats and other leisure vehicles. Discuss the pro's and con's of leisure activities that use petroleum: car races, tractor pulls, parades, and so on.

6. Design ways to keep track of family car usage and cut down on short trips. [grocery lists for weekly shopping, planning ahead, and so on.]

7. How do the relative costs of various materials and methods affect the use of these in removing oil from the environment?

Facilitator _____

Timer _____

Reporter _____

Encourager _____

Don't Cry Over Spilled Oil

Your Predictions:

1. From the list below, what do you think will do the best job of removing the oil from the materials?

_____

Why? _____

2. Test your predictions.

Materials used to remove oil	Description of what happened
paper towels	
cotton balls	
yarn	
string	
spoons	
liquid detergent	

What worked best for your group? _____

What worked best in the whole class? _____

What did you learn? _____

9   Kalah, An Ancient Game

Focus

Students learn to play the Middle Eastern game of Kalah as a way of learning about the culture of that region.

Resources

For each pair of students:
1 standard 12-hole (2 x 6) egg carton, preferably styrofoam
scissors or dull serrated knife
stapler or tape
36 dried lima beans or smooth stones
scrap paper for scoring

Background

Kalah seems to be one of the oldest games in the world. It is thought to have begun in the Middle East, although it has been very popular throughout Africa in various forms. In the ruins of ancient cities, carved stone Kalah games and paintings of people playing Kalah have been found.

Evidently Kalah was played under all types of circumstances. In some tribes only the king and a chosen opponent could play, while the rest of the tribe would stand around and watch. It is said that one maharajah in India was so wealthy that his playing pieces were diamonds and rubies! When a traveling caravan stopped for the night, people might make twelve small holes in the sand and play. Small boys would also make a board this way. In such situations the players would use shells or smooth stones for the playing pieces.

Kalah, as it is known in the Middle East, or *Mankala*, as it is known in Africa, is still popular. Recently, in Africa, someone purchased a very ornate carved elephant with the game board carved in its back.

Kalah is definitely a skill-based game, as opposed to the many chance-based games played most often today. In Kalah, as in some games like chess and checkers, the players control the action by the way they move the playing pieces. Students should know this, so that they expect to spend some time learning how to play the game; they will be frustrated and disappointed if they expect instant gratification! This, however, is a distinct advantage of having students learn to play Kalah: to develop any degree of skill at all in playing in the game, they will have to exercise decision-making, problem solving, and mental-math abilities.

Teaching Tips

1. Here are directions for making the game board:

   - Cut off the long tab of the egg carton.
   - Cut off the lid.
   - Cut the lid crosswise into 2 pieces.
   - Staple or tape the lid halves to the ends of the carton, making sure that the lid pieces project out far enough to produce trays or *kalahs*. Stuff a small piece of paper down into the openings, where the kalahs meet the main part of the carton, to keep the playing pieces in the kalahs. (You may prefer to use two small (separate) cups for kalahs.)

Procedure

1. Two players sit opposite one another with the game between them.

2. Learn the terms used in the game:
   pit:: one cup of the egg carton (There are 12 pits in all. The 6 nearest to you are yours.)
   kalah: a larger cup or section on either end (There are two kalahs, one for each player; your kalah is on your right.)
   beans:: playing pieces (Smooth stones or even buttons may be substituted.)
   The row of pits in front of you are your own pits.

3. Place 3 game pieces in each of the 12 pits.

4. Each pair of players decide who will play first; one selects *even*, and the other, *odd*. Each picks up any number of beans without the other seeing. On a given signal, they both show how many beans they have drawn. If the total is even, the player that chose *even* plays first, but if odd, the player that chose odd plays first.

5. Begin the game by picking up all of the beans in any one of your own pits. Drop the beans one at a time in the pits beginning in the pit immediately to the right of the one which was just emptied and continuing counter-clockwise until all of the beans held are distributed. If you reach or pass your own kalah, drop a bean into that also. Remember, however, that if you ever reach or pass your opponent's kalah, you must <u>not</u> drop one of your beans into it.

6. Your turn now ends unless one of these things happens. If your last bean drops into your own kalah, you get another turn. If your last bean drops into an empty pit on your side of the board, you capture your opponent's beans in the pit

opposite. Put these and the last bean played in your kalah; then your turn ends).

7. Take turns in this manner until one player wins the round by emptying all of his or her pits. The player with beans remaining in the pits gives them to the winner.

8. Find the difference between the total beans in the kalahs of the two players; this is the winner's point score for the round.

9. The loser plays first in the next round.

10. The player reaching 40 points first wins the game.

11. Use these questions in a class discussion:

   • What do you think ancient people used instead of egg cartons and beans?
   • Why do you think ancient people enjoyed playing games like kalah? What does this tell us about them? Why do we play games?
   • Suppose two people were angry with each other and then they played a game like Kalah. What do you think might happen?
   • What are some other games that you enjoy playing? Why do you enjoy playing them?

Try This

1. Increase the number of beans in each pit to begin with.

2. Try to keep from getting points. The one who reaches 10 first loses.

3. Play with partners.

4. Try using two egg cartons, placed end-to-end, using 24 pits .

5. Help students improve their thinking skills by having them write out the directions in proper sequence.

6. Have students devise ways of making the point-scoring system more complicated. For example, you could assign an odd number of points, like 38.5, to each bean; other ways would be to increase the number of beans in each pit or allow the two players to determine how each of them would distribute 18 beans.

7. Find a way to make a kalah game of other materials or decorate the one you have. In some countries they carve the Kalah board out of wood.

Kalah

The Oldest Game in the World

You will need an egg carton.

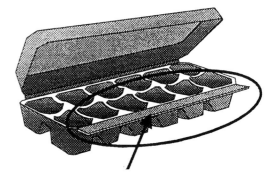

(1) Cut off the tab.

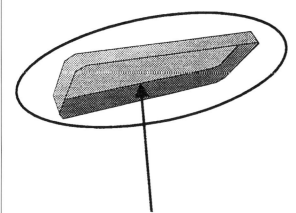

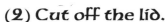

(2) Cut off the lid.

(3) Cut the lid into 2 equal parts.

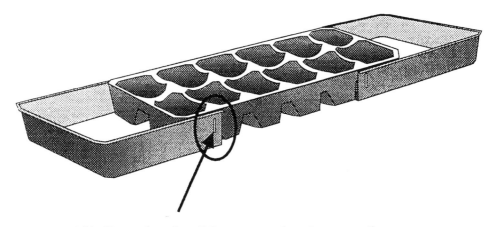

(4) Staple the lid onto the base of the carton.

10   Islamic Geometric Designs

Focus

Students construct geometric designs with circles, a basic pattern of artistic design in Islamic cultures.

Resources

For the class:
articles or pictures of articles with geometric designs (oriental rugs, mosaics, pictures of mosques, and so on)

For each student:
good quality mechanical drawing compass or circle template
straight-edge (ruler)
paper (can be scrap for practice)
colored pens or pencils, preferably with fairly sharp points

Background

While it is not strictly against Islamic religious law to represent humans and animals pictorially, the teachings of Muhammed against idolatry have been interpreted this way by some Muslim leaders. This and other factors led to the emergence of *pattern* in Islamic art. These patterns were arabesques (derived from plant life), calligraphy, and the repetition of geometric elements (the idea applied in this activity).

Photo courtesy of Aramco World

Islamic geometric patterns in this activity have five basic characteristics:

1. They are composed of repeated geometric shapes.
2. They radiate symmetrically from a central point.
3. They are designed to continue indefinitely.
4. They are based on a grid of equilateral triangles or squares called *tessellations*, constructed from patterns of circles.
5. They are two-dimensional.

Teaching Tips

1. In using the compass to draw circles, be sure students maintain the same radius by tracing pennies.

2. This is a good activity for helping students learn to follow directions and do careful work! They must plan each set of points before drawing circles.

3. It helps to color a design as you go.

Procedure

1. Fold a square of paper in half; open it up and fold it a second time from the opposite side.

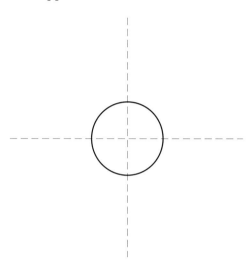

Photo courtesy of Aramco World

2. Set the compass for a diameter of less than one inch. Place the compass point on the intersection of the folds and draw a circle.

3. Lift the compass, keeping the diameter the same. Make colored dots on the four points where the inscribed circle intersects the fold lines. Using each of these points as a center, inscribe four intersecting circles.

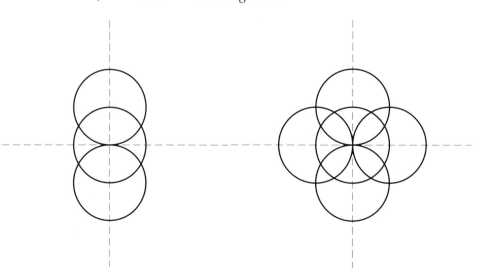

4. Now mark the four (outermost) points where the circles intersect. (Note the other intersections that you could use as centers another time.) Draw 4 more circles using these points as centers.

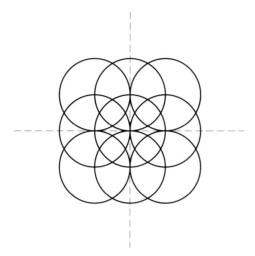

5. At this point you may proceed in any number of ways. Here are a few:

   - Continue to make dots and draw circles in a regular design. Color later.
   - Begin to color in a pattern, starting at the center. Let the colored lines guide your pattern.
   - Begin to draw colored lines between the points where intersecting lines meet.
   - Begin to draw black lines between the points where intersecting lines meet. Later, color the geometric shapes or segments you have outlined.

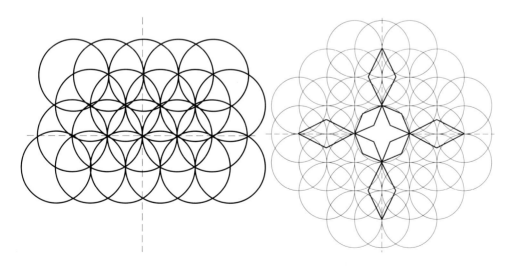

6. Allow students to explore and experiment with designs. However you wish to work, guide students to locate hidden patterns, such as triangle grids, hexagons, or the optical illusion of stacked blocks. Have students examine the articles and pictures to see how the designs were built geometrically.

7. Discuss students' experiences.

   • Why do you think geometric designs like this become popular?
   • How do you think these designs were used? [pottery; textiles; mosaic floors, walls, and ceilings]

Try This

1. Instead of using the four points where the original circle intersects the fold lines, divide the original circle into six segments with the compass diameter. Use these points to construct six-sided designs.

2. Have groups work together to produce a larger scale design. For this you may wish to tape the paper to a table.

3. *Art/architecture:* Try to locate slides or videotapes of Islamic art and architecture at a local library or a nearby college. Find geometric or other types of art. Try to duplicate some of the designs.

4. *Art:* Transfer the geometric designs drawn in the activity to tiles; paint or glaze appropriately.

5. *Math:* Study the geometry involved in the designs: the shapes, the size of the angles, and so on.

Photo courtesy of Aramco World

11   Miniature Painting

Focus

Students will gain an appreciation for Iranian miniature painting by using the same techniques.

Resources (see *Teaching Tips*)

For each student:
1 1/2 inch round pearl button
paint (see *Teaching Tips*)
round <u>and</u> flat toothpicks for each color of paint
pin or magnet for back of button

For the class:
glue gun or craft glue
Fix-It or other matte finish spray

newspapers to protect table
plasticene clay, piece the size of a golf ball
colored markers
small pieces of tissue for "erasing" mistakes
optional: small paint brushes (see Teaching Tips)

Background

Painting in miniature can be traced back to the sixth century, when the first Islamic school of miniature painting was established in what is now the country we call Turkey. These oldest miniature paintings were done on highly polished paper using paint pigment mixed with white of egg. Many such paintings with intricate detail illustrated epic poems and books of love and war heroism. Over the next three hundred years, the popularity of painting small figures in brilliant colors seems to have spread to Persia.

One of the earliest miniature paintings on pottery is a Persian twelfth-century goblet. From this time onward, miniature painting was used as an art form and was not limited to book illustration. In Persia, the small paintings often told of Rustam, a legendary hero who constantly upheld standards of righteousness and justice.

During the seventeenth century, the Mongol tribes invaded the Middle East. Since they brought craftsmen and artists with them, the style of miniature painting and other art forms were admired and taken back to India and China.

Near the end of the eighteenth century, several changes took place which brought about the decline of miniature painting. For one thing, increased contact with Europe meant an increased interest in oil paintings, most of which were done on large canvases. Also, the printing press was adapted to utilize Arabic characters in 1727. This resulted in a gradual decline in the number of illustrated manuscripts which included miniature painting. However, miniature painting is still taught at the Academy of Fine Arts in Istanbul.

When we think of something being miniature, we tend to expect it to be tiny. Some painting called miniature was not as small as what is done in this activity. Of course, they were probably considered miniature by Europeans in comparison to the huge canvases on which oil paintings were done.

Teaching Tips

1. Obtain paint from a craft store. We used *Ceramcoat* by *Delta*, but any artists' acrylic, water base paint will do. If students work quickly, a group can share a bit of each color of paint poured into bottle caps. Otherwise, each group will need bottles. It does dry fast!

2. Beforehand, accumulate magazine and greeting card landscapes. Especially for students' first projects, most will want something to copy or at least follow. Pictures with people, animals, and trees are most suitable.

3. As you will see in producing a sample painting, it takes a bit of practice to apply the paint in a pleasing manner. Allow enough time for students to practice. They need especially to learn how to use the sides and edges of the flat toothpick, and the end of either kind of toothpick does not hold much paint! You may wish to try small paint brushes; the Persians used brushes with one goat or camel hair for fine work.

Procedure

1. Let class members share information about miniatures. Some may know someone who builds miniature cars or doll house furniture. Weave into the discussion and the rest of the activity the information in the *Background* section.

2. On the activity sheets, each student designs a simple scene, first in the larger circle and then in miniature.

3. Press the button into the ball of clay, so that it will be easy to hold while you paint. Mark clay with your initials.

4. Paint the scene on the button. Work slowly and carefully. Commend those using patience.

5. When finished, press clay ball on table or a tray, so that it will not roll over. Set aside for paint to dry.

6. When dry, spray to make it waterproof.

7. Turn button over and glue on pin or magnet

8. Allow time to admire one another's project and to build an appreciation for this ancient art. This would be a good time to talk about how much patience people would have to have if they did this all the time. Take photos or videotape finished projects.

Try This

1. If your students are able, compute the relative area of the large and small circles, to give the scale of the miniature paintings you are doing. Make up some problems based on this.

2. Research what would be Middle Eastern to use in paintings: trees, flowers, houses, people's dress, and so on.

3. Make a book of poetry, illustrating the first letter of each poem. Find pictures of ancient illustrated manuscripts.

The jewelry pictured was made in Iran in the 1960's. It is done in oil paint on mother-of-pearl, framed in a silver-colored metal.

Here's an enlarged view of a link of the bracelet. This link is actually 2 cm wide and 2.5 cm high.

Try Some Miniature Painting!

In ancient Turkey, over a thousand years ago, artists started painting beautiful miniature pictures. At first they painted on paper, decorating hand-printed poems and stories. Later, in Persia (present Iran), they painted scenes on bowls, vases, and goblets.

Plan your miniature painting by drawing it in a large circle. Then try painting it in miniature in a small circle. Here are some circles for you to use for practice.

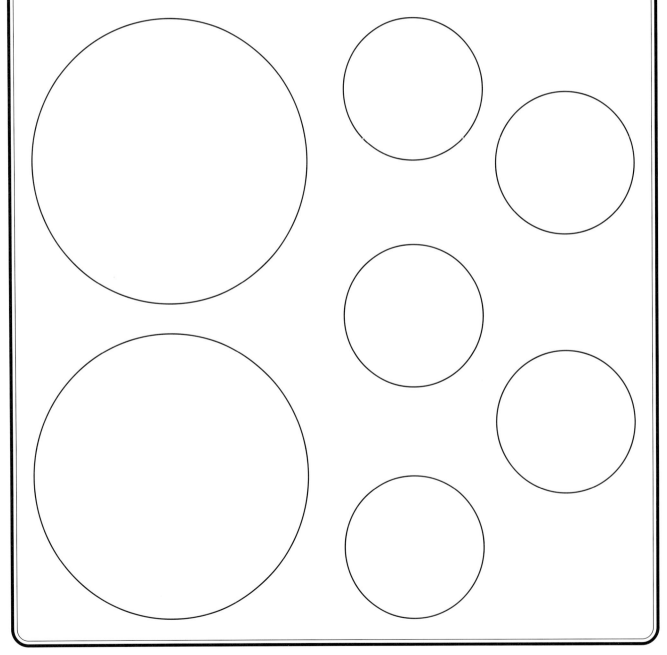

12   Three Faiths

Focus

Students will play a bingo-type game, with each round focusing on one of the three major faiths followed in the Middle East: Judaism, Christianity, or Islam.

Resources

For each pair of students:
8.5" x 11" paper or game form
2 markers, 1 red and 1 blue

For the teacher or game leader:
2 markers, 1 red and 1 blue

Background

In present-day schools, teachers are encouraged to teach students regarding the major faiths, but it is often difficult to do this without serious controversies. This activity avoids such comparison and interpretation difficulties by dealing only with the basic facts related to each faith and by keeping the three faiths separate; students play a separate round of the game for each faith. In this way, there need not be any comparison of the three faiths.

The nature of the activity requires brief answers; this sometimes has the unfortunate effect of oversimplification. The Jewish Sabbath, for example, lasts from sundown Friday to sundown Saturday, but the answer given is "Saturday." Keep in mind that the goal is to teach a few basic facts about the three major faiths.

Here is a brief summary of the history of the three faiths:

Judaism

Judaism began 4000 years ago in what is today called Israel. Jews believe that God created the world and that Abraham, who came from Ur in Mesopotamia, was chosen by God to be one of his messengers. Abraham and his wife Sarah journeyed from Mesopotamia to Canaan (Palestine) and there had a son, Isaac. Since

Abraham was obedient to God, he was promised that a Messiah or Savior would come from his descendants. Modern Jews still look forward to the coming of the Messiah. Isaac's grandsons became the leaders of the twelve tribes of the Hebrews, from which Jews believe they are descended. Moses is revered as another messenger of God who led the Hebrews out of slavery in Egypt; this is still commemorated in the annual Passover feast. Moses received from God the Ten Commandments, contained in the Torah (the books of the Law). The *halakha* is the Jewish religious law which supplements Scripture.

The Jews believe they have a covenant with God that if they obey the commandments, He will protect them as his chosen people. Today there are 1.3 million Jews.

Christianity

Traditional Christians believe that God created the world as the Bible describes. They also believe that about 2000 years ago, a baby named Jesus was born to a Jewish woman in Bethlehem, Palestine. He was the Messiah, the Son of God, whom the Jewish Scriptures had predicted. They also believe that He was sent to earth to redeem humanity and bring peace on earth by His death and resurrection. Followers of Jesus became the first Christians.

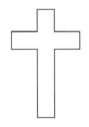

Modern Christians accept the Old Testament (the Jewish Scriptures), but they also believe that many prophecies there are fulfilled by the coming of Jesus Christ and other events described in the New Testament (the writings of the followers of Jesus Christ). Modern Christians observe the birth of Jesus at Christmas and His resurrection at Easter. They worship each Sunday to commemorate the Resurrection. There are about 1.6 billion people in the world that call themselves Christians, although for many of these this means they are neither Jews nor Muslims.

Islam

Muslims believe that they are descendants of Abraham and his slave Hagar, through his son Ishmael. They believe that God created the world as the Bible describes, and they accept the Old Testament as a historical account. In A.D. 622, Mohammed, a special prophet of God, was born. He received a message from God or Allah through the archangel Gabriel, a message recorded in the Quran (Koran). Muslims believe that Abraham, Moses, and Jesus were important messengers of God.

Muslims pray five times a day, facing Mecca, Saudi Arabia, the place of Mohammed's birth. The month of Ramadan commemorates the revelation of the archangel Gabriel to Mohammed. During Ramadan, Muslims fast during the day and feast at night. Jerusalem is sacred to Muslims because it is the site of Mohammed's ascension into heaven. Medina, Saudi Arabia, is also sacred because Mohammed's tomb is there. If possible, faithful Muslims make a journey to Mecca at least once in their lives. They must also give to the poor. There are about 860 million Muslims throughout the world.

Teaching Tips

1. This activity consists of three separate rounds, one for each major faith. Teachers who have field-tested this game say that it is both enjoyable and profitable to play all three rounds more than once.

2. Playing the game in pairs allows students to work together cooperatively.

3. Students and the leader use the red markers to number answers; then, when players have four in a row, they use blue markers to check correct answers.

Rules of the Game

1. Students, in pairs, fold a blank sheet of paper into sixteen squares and label any one square FREE.

2. Given an answer sheet of fifteen facts, students record each one in any square.

3. Play begins when the teacher, using the question and answer sheet, reads any question aloud. The teacher notes the question in red as number one.

4. Students find what they think is the correct answer to the question. They place a red "X" and also the number of the question in that square. Allow 15 seconds for finding answers.

Photo courtesy of Aramco World

These children carry Ramadan lanterns as they hope their singing will bring them sweet rewards.

5. Play continues in this way. until a pair of students has marked four squares in a row.

6. Check the answers of the winning student(s). The students call out the number in the each square and the answer marked there. The teacher reads the corresponding question, and the class decides whether or not the answer is correct. Keep discussions factual.

7. Whenever an answer is deemed to be incorrect, the checking stops immediately and play continues until the next pair wins. If answers are correct, this pair is declared the winners; their reward is to lead the game and ask the questions until all questions have been asked. This means, unfortunately, that at least a few students will find, toward the end of the game, that their available answers cannot possibly answer the questions being asked.

8. Play continues until all fifteen facts are marked. Discuss answers and share information.

9. If desired, you may see who has the most correct answers in total.

Extra Questions for Larger Charts

1. Why is Jerusalem important to this religion?
   - J: Jerusalem is the City of David and site of Solomon's temple.
   - C: Jerusalem is the site of Christ's death and resurrection.
   - I: Jerusalem is the site of Mohammed's ascension.

2. What is the significance of their major religious observances?
   - J: At Passover, they commemorate their release from slavery in Egypt.
   - C: At Christmas, they commemorate the birth of Jesus Christ; at Easter they remember His death and resurrection.
   - I: At Ramadan, they commemorate the visitation of the archangel Gabriel, bearing Allah's word to Mohammed.

3. What writings best summarize the beliefs of this religion?
   - J: They try to keep the Ten Commandments.
   - C: They believe that John 3:16, the Ten Commandments, and the Sermon on the Mount are all important.
   - I: They try to practice the Five Pillars of Islam.

4. What do followers look forward to?
   - J: They look forward to coming of the Messiah.
   - C: They look forward to everlasting life with God in heaven and also to the second coming of Jesus Christ.
   - I: They look forward to everlasting life in Paradise.

5. Name a ritual important to followers?
   - J: Boys are circumcised. When boys and girls are twelve years old, They become adults in a bar mitzvah (for boys) or bas mitzvah (for girls) ceremony.
   - C: They obey Jesus Christ's command to take communion to remember Him.
   - M: They pray five times a day, facing Mecca.

6. Are there any dietary laws?
   - J: They eat kosher food and no pork
   - C: Many drink no alcohol.
   - I: They eat no pork and drink no alcohol.

Photo courtesy of Aramco World

The Dome of the Rock in Jerusalem is a mosque, a Muslim place of worship.

Leader's Key - Judaism

1.	What is the name of this faith?	Judaism
2.	What are the followers of Judaism called?	Jews
3.	Who is called the father of Judaism?	Abraham
4.	Name a significant person in the history of Judaism.	Moses
5.	What is the historical name of God in Judaism?	Yahweh
6.	What is the sacred text of Judaism?	Torah
7.	What do Jews call their place of worship?	synagogue
8.	On what day of the week do Jews worship?	Saturday
9.	Name an important holy time for Jews.	Passover
10.	What is the symbol of Judaism?	Star of David
11.	What is the most sacred city to followers of Judaism?	Jerusalem
12.	What do Jews call their religious leader?	rabbi
13.	Name a children's religious ceremony of Judaism.	bar mitzvah
14.	Are there any diet limitations for Jews?	no pork, kosher rules
15.	Who do they think created the world?	God

Leader's Key - Christianity

1.	What is the name of this religion?	Christianity
2.	What are followers of Christianity called?	Christians
3.	How does Christianity trace its roots?	Jewish scriptures
4.	How do Christians speak of Jesus Christ?	Saviour
5.	What is the name of God in Christianity?	Lord
6.	What is the sacred text of Christianity?	Bible
7.	What do Christians call their place of worship?	church
8.	On what day of the week do Christians worship?	Sunday
9.	Name an important holy time for Christians.	Easter
10.	What is the symbol of Christianity?	cross
11.	Name an important city.	Jerusalem
12.	What is a Christian religious leader called?	pastor
13.	Name an important Christian ceremony.	baptism
14.	Who do they think created the world?	God
15.	Are there any diet limitations for Christians?	none

Leader's Key - Islam

1.	What is the name of this religion?	Islam
2.	What are followers of Islam called?	Muslims
3.	How does Islam trace its way back to Abraham?	Christianity and Judaism
4.	Who is the most significant person in Islam?	Mohammed
5.	What is the name of God in Islam?	Allah
6.	What is the sacred text of Islam?	Quran or Koran
7.	What do Muslims call their place of worship?	mosque
8.	On what day of the week do Muslims worship?	Friday
9.	Name an important holy time in Islam.	Ramadan
10.	What is the symbol of Islam?	star and crescent moon
11.	Name a city which is sacred to Muslims.	Mecca
12.	What do Muslims call their religious leaders?	imam
13.	Who do they think created the world?	God
14.	Name two modern groups of Muslims.	Sunni or Shiite
15.	Are there any diet limitations for Muslims?	no pork or alcohol

Student Answer Sheet

Judaism	Christianity	Islam
Judaism.	Christianity	Islam
Jews	Christians	Muslims
Abraham	Jewish Scriptures	Judaism and Christianity
Moses	Saviour	Mohammed
Yahweh	Lord	Allah
Torah	Bible	Koran
synagogue	church	mosque
Saturday	Sunday	Friday
Passover	Easter	Ramadan
Star of David	cross	star and crescent moon
Jerusalem	Jerusalem	Mecca
rabbi	pastor	imam
bar mitzvah	baptism	God
God	God	Sunni, Shiite
no pork, kosher rules	none	no pork, no alcohol

Three Faiths

Name _____

Faith _____

13   A Taste of the Middle East

Focus

Students will learn about common foods and eating customs of the Middle East by eating some typical foods and observing customs related to hospitality.

Resources

For the class:
    ingredients for recipes you wish to use, plus
        kitchen utensils for preparing and serving them
    finger foods: olives, dried fruit: dates, raisins, figs, or
        apricots
    thermal pitcher or other way to serve hot mint tea

For each student:
    pillow, preferably large
    sturdy paper plate
    hot cup
    large paper napkin

For each group of 6-8 students:
    small rug
    carafe, pitcher, or jar (for handwashing)
    10"-12" diameter bowl (for handwashing)

Background

Religious faith has been a strong factor in what people of the region eat. For ancient Israelites and modern orthodox Jews, the dietary laws in the Bible (mainly in the Book of Leviticus) forbid the eating of certain foods because they are not considered clean or healthful. People may not eat blood or the meat of animals that have died of natural causes (chapter 17). They are to eat meat from only those animals that chew the cud <u>and</u> have divided hooves, such as cattle, sheep, and goats; thus, the laws eliminate the eating of pork, camel, or rabbit (chapter 11). Other animals, fish, birds, and even insects are identified as clean and unclean.

Photo courtesy of Aramco World

Although orthodox Christians accept the Bible as an authority, they do not follow the dietary laws of the Old Testament. They believe that the New Testament and the teachings of Jesus Christ frees them from the limitations of Old Testament law. "...food does not bring us near to God" (I Corinthians, chapter 8).

In the Koran, Muslims are commanded not to eat swine or pork (Sura II: Baqara). As with Jewish people, they may not eat meat from animals that have died of natural causes. Also, they may not eat any food which has been offered to idols or false gods.

Teaching Tips

1. Many of the foods mentioned are available at delicatessens or food stores serving Oriental needs. For an authentic touch, you may wish to purchase some foods (like baklava) ready-made, although it is much less expensive to make. If possible, use phylo leaves (thin sheets of pastry) that have not been frozen. If desired, small tasting-sized portions may be placed on cupcake papers.

2. This activity portrays a Middle Eastern village meal; in the cities, especially in modern times, many people eat Western-style at tables, using silverware.

3. An authentic meal would have dishes of food on the rug or on a low table in the center of a family or other group, as shown. Those eating would pick up finger foods or dip pieces of bread into large bowls of stew-like mixtures and salad. For hygiene reasons, this classroom activity has been adapted to provide individual portions.

4. Here are some pointers for making baklava:

   - The process is easiest if size of pan is close to that of phylo leaves.
   - Keep phylo leaves on waxed paper or plastic tray while working.
   - Use a wide, flat pastry brush or 1-inch, clean paintbrush.
   - Cover phylo leaves with flat-woven towel, not terrycloth, while working.
   - To make baklava crisper and fluffier (rather than chewy), clarify butter by simmering it 20 minutes on very low heat. Cool slightly ; then remove salty foam from the top and use only the liquid.

5. The carafe and bowl are for handwashing, which should be done <u>before and after</u> the meal. (Long ago, this and footwashing would have rinsed off the traveler's dust and sand; the small containers are reminders that water is precious in this region.) Each "guest" holds hands palms-up, while the host pours a small amount of water (probably about one-fourth cup or less) onto them. The bowl should be large enough that as the guest rubs hands together, the bowl catches the excess water.

6. For the mint tea, place fresh mint leaves in a large jar and cover with boiling water; let steep ten minutes and sweeten with honey. You may also use commercially-prepared mint tea bags, dried mint, or mint extract.

7. NOTE: Have all students wash their hands <u>with soap</u> before preparing or eating food. The handwashing included in the activity is largely ceremonial, even in the Middle East; it is a sign of hospitality.

8. Decide beforehand how authentic you want to be. Here are some examples of authentic (and then simplified) food choices:

Appetizers:
- Hummus dip (recipe provided) with pita bread bits
- Olives, pickles
- Inch-sized chunks of cucumber, tomato, turnip, beet, chilis

Main dishes:
- Lentil soup
- Hummus in pita bread, topped with lettuce and tomato (like a taco!)
- Roast chicken stuffed with ground lamb and rice
- Baked fish with tomatoes, onions, lemon juice, parsley
- Stew made of lamb and vegetables, seasoned with cumin

Salads:
- Tabbouleh
- Chunks of tomatoes and cucumbers with olive oil and lemon juice

Desserts:
- Fresh fruit: apples, grapes, watermelon, pomegranates
- Dried fruits: dates, figs, apricots, raisins
- Pudding
- Baklava or other pastry

Suggestions for a simplified sampling menu:
- Lentil soup (small cup—it's filling!)
- Half-round (or less) of pita bread with hummus
- Tabbouleh
- Rice pudding (small cup)
- Mint tea

Procedure

1. Plan your menu, beforehand or with students. Adapt recipes as needed to allow for finicky tastes! <u>Plan for small portions, with refills for those who enjoy the various foods.</u>

2. Prepare foods, and arrange in serving portions as planned (see *Teaching Tips*, above).

3. Arrange the room as shown, with pillows and small rugs to accommodate groups of five or six students, with a "host" for each group. Assign students to groups.

4. Guests go outside the classroom or to one side of the room, while hosts stand near their "homes" (rugs). Hosts and guests greet one another by bowing heads. Guests sit down on the floor, each person sitting on or leaning onto a pillow, as shown. Leave a pillow and space in each group for the host.

5. Hosts perform the handwashing, described above in the *Teaching Tips* section. No towels are used; so little water is needed that guests let hands dry naturally.

6. Hosts serve the food and a cup of mint tea to each guest in the group, both bowing the head as this is done. When all have been served and host is seated, guests eat the food and talk quietly. This would be a good time to point out the differences between this and an authentic Middle Eastern meal in a village.

7. Hosts perform handwashing a second time before guests leave.

8. Share and discuss students' reactions to the activity:

   • If you had walked all day across the desert, how do you think the handwashing would make you feel?
   • Which of these foods are also foods that we eat? [point out how many of the foods are the same.]
   • Do you think the people eat a healthful diet?
   • Why do you think the people sit on the floor? [scarcity of wood or other materials for making furniture]
   • How many of these foods do you think are raised in the Middle East? [all]
   • Which of the foods tasted best to you?

Try This

1. Encourage students to ask at home about Middle Eastern foods and recipes their families may know.

2. Find out what spices are used in Middle Eastern foods. Where do they come from? Long ago, how did these spices reach the Middle East?

3. Find out more about oases, what life is like and what foods grow there.

A Taste of the Middle East

Baklava (makes over 50 pieces of pastry)   Oven 325°

Syrup: *Pastry:*
2 c. sugar   1 lb. pkg. phylo leaves (24-30 leaves)
1 1/2 c. water   1/2 lb. butter
1 tsp. lemon juice   2 c. walnuts, finely chopped
                                  1/2 tsp. cinnamon
                                  2 Tbsp. brown sugar

Make the syrup first. Combine the sugar and water; bring to a rolling boil. Boil 10 minutes or until it is syrupy, stirring often. Remove from heat and stir in the lemon juice. Set aside to cool. Preheat oven. In a bowl, combine nuts, brown sugar, and cinnamon; set aside. Melt the butter; brush some on the bottom and sides of a baking dish at least 10" x 14." Spread out phylo leaves on tray or counter, and cover with very damp dish towel, as phylo dries out quickly. Carefully place one phylo leaf in the pan, folding down any edges; immediately cover the rest with the towel. Brush the whole phylo leaf with butter, edges first. (Do not be too generous or you will not have enough butter.)

Continue adding leaves and buttering until you have used half the phylo leaves. Spread nuts evenly over the pastry. Cover with the remaining phylo leaves, buttering them one at a time, as before. <u>Be sure you save enough butter to be generous on the second-last and last phylos; this makes cutting easier.</u> When all layers are complete, use a sharp knife or pizza cutter to cut dough into diamond-shaped pieces. (Cut the width into strips 1 1/2 inches wide and then cut diagonally across the strips.) <u>Butter the top of each piece well.</u>

Bake 30-35 minutes until puffed and lightly browned, watching carefully. Spoon cooled syrup all over the hot pastry. Serve at room temperature—with plenty of napkins!

Tabbouleh (Wheat, Mint, and Parsley Salad)

1/2 c. bulghur wheat, finely cracked	dash salt
3 med. tomatoes, in small pieces	1/3 c. lemon juice
2 c. fresh parsley	1/3 c. olive oil
1/2 c. fresh mint leaves	dash pepper or allspice
1 med. cucumber	romaine or lettuce leaves

optional: 1 chopped green onion or 1/2 tsp. dried green onion

Place bulghur in bowl. Cover well with boiling water and set aside for 15 minutes or until soft, like oatmeal. Meanwhile, remove stems from parsley and mint, and peel cucumber (optional to remove seeds); chop all of these fine. When bulghur is soft, drain in sieve, press out extra water, and replace in bowl. Add remaining ingredients. Stir. Chill for at least a half hour. To serve, line salad bowl with romaine or lettuce leaves and add tabbouleh.

Rice Pudding

1 c. water
1 qt. milk (can be skim)
1 c. short- or medium-grain rice (not minute variety)
1/3 c. sugar
1 tsp. almond or vanilla flavoring
cinnamon or cinnamon-sugar mixture
optional: 1/2 c. raisins or chopped pistachio nuts

In a saucepan combine water and rice. Bring to a boil and then boil on medium heat about 5 minutes or until almost all of the water has been absorbed. Heat the milk almost to a boil and gradually stir it in. Lower heat to simmer and note the time. Simmer about 10 minutes, stirring slowly and only enough to prevent rice from clumping or sticking to the bottom of the pot. When the mixture starts to thicken, stir in sugar and flavoring. Remove from heat. Cover and let sit for 10 minutes. Pour into casserole or serving dishes. Sprinkle with cinnamon-sugar and garnish with raisins or nuts. (makes 5 cups)

Hummus

1 16-oz. can garbanzo beans (chick peas)	2 cloves garlic
3 Tbsp. lemon juice	dash. salt
1-2 Tbsp. tahini or sesame seed oil	1 tsp. olive oil
garnish: paprika, pine nuts, and fresh parsley	pita bread

Drain beans but save the liquid. In a blender or food processor place half the liquid, the beans, lemon juice, garlic, tahini, and salt. Puree to form a smooth paste about the consistency of peanut butter, adding more liquid if necessary. Add to taste the cumin or additional lemon juice.

To serve: (1) For a lunch, cut pita bread in half, and fill with 2 Tbsp. of hummus; add tabbouleh or tomatoes and lettuce. (2) For a snack or appetizer, spread on a large plate or platter, smoothing with the back of a spoon. Drizzle olive oil on top. Sprinkle paprika in the center and garnish around the edge with chopped nuts and parsley. Serve with pita bread, which is torn into small pieces for dipping.

Lentil Soup (makes about a half-gallon of thick soup)

8 c. water or chicken stock	6 med. cloves garlic
1 1/2 c. dried lentils	1 1/2 c. chopped carrots
1/4 tsp. pepper	2 c. onions, chopped
1 Tbsp. olive oil	1 1/2 c. celery, with leaves
3 Tbsp. dried or fresh parsley	

1 14-oz. can tomatoes
2 tsp. salt
1 tsp. basil
1 tsp. marjoram
optional: 4-6 chicken bouillon cubes

Wash and drain lentils. In a large pot combine water, lentils, pepper, and olive oil; bring to a boil and note time. Cover, simmer, and start chopping and adding the vegetables, covering between additions: garlic, carrots, onions, celery, and then tomatoes. Stir occasionally to be sure the soup doesn't stick to the bottom of the pot; add water if too thick. Add salt and spices, plus bouillon cubes if not using chicken stock. Before serving add the parsley (so it will stay green). Stir the soup as you serve it, because the lentils tend to sink to the bottom.

14   Middle Eastern Foods

Resource Sheet

In ancient Mesopotamia, people learned to plant crops; they also tamed animals and raised them for food. Early Sumerians, Babylonians, and Egyptians entertained at lavish banquets. As they expanded their empires and traded with India, China, and Europe, they learned to enjoy new foods and new flavors. The resulting Middle Eastern cuisine is a unique mixture of foods and food customs from all over the neighboring continents.

Religious faith has been a factor in what foods people of the region eat. For ancient Israelites and modern orthodox Jews, the dietary laws in the Bible forbid the eating of pork and certain other foods because they are not considered clean or healthful. Although orthodox Christians accept the whole Bible as an authority, they believe that the New Testament and the teachings of Jesus Christ free Christians from obeying dietary laws given in what they call the Old Testament. Because of instructions in the Koran, orthodox Muslims do not eat pork or certain other foods.

Because it has always been expensive, meat is eaten only on special occasions. The diet of most people in the Middle East (especially in the villages) consists mainly of grains (such as rice, wheat, and barley) and dried legumes (such as garbanzo beans and lentils). Lunches and meals eaten while on-the-job or traveling might be hummus (pureed garbanzo beans or chick-peas) in pita or pocket bread, topped like a taco with tomato and shredded lettuce. Bread is considered a basic daily food and is consumed at every meal. Pita bread is made in different sizes; people place food inside it (as in a sandwich or tortilla) or tear pieces from it to scoop up other foods. Yogurt is also popular; people make their own.

When a bit of meat is added to vegetable and grain stew-like mixtures, it is usually lamb, although fish, chicken, beef, goat, and even camel meat are also eaten. The flavor is often enhanced with the spices for which the Middle East is famous. The most plentiful fresh vegetables include eggplant, olives, tomatoes, beans, zucchini, spinach, parsley, and artichokes. Salads are popular, even at breakfast! Lemon juice and olive oil are often used as a delicious salad dressing.

Desserts are simple, usually fruit or some pudding. Rich pastries like baklava are served only on special occasions. Mint tea or strong Arabic coffee (very sweet and often spiced with cardamom) completes the meal.

15 Our Middle Eastern Heritage

Resource Sheet

Many things we see and use every day were discovered or developed in the Middle East. Muslim mathematicians and scientists preserved and translated many ancient writings from Greek, Persian, Syriac, and other languages into Arabic. They worked to correct errors (their own and others') and to explain for the first time such basic procedures as the scientific method. Most of this work started about A.D. 600 and ended in A.D. 1258 when Baghdad was captured by the Mongols. Here are some of the major gifts the peole of the Middle East have given to us:

Photo courtesy of Aramco World

Here are some English words that have come to us from the Arabic language.*

admiral	borax	gauze	ream
adobe	caliber	ghoul	retina
alchemy	candy	gypsum	saffron
alcohol	carafe	hazard	sash
alcove	caraway	jar	satin
alfalfa	cataract	jasmine	sherbet
algebra	check	julep	sofa
algorism	check-mate	lute	sugar
alkali	chiffon	macabre	sumac
almanac	cipher	magazine	syrup
arsenal;	coffee	magnet	taffeta
atlas	cornea	marzipan	tambourine
average	cotton	mattress	tariff
azure	crimson	mohair	traffic
baroque	damask	muslin	zenith
barracks	elixir	racquet	zero

* taken from the *Arab World Notebook*

- These are foods that originally came to us from the Middle East:*

  apricots
  artichokes
  asparagus
  bananas
  buckwheat
  cherries
  dates
  eggplant
  figs
  ginger
  grapefruit
  lemons
  limes
  oranges
  pomegranates
  quinces
  rice
  scallions
  spinach
  strawberries
  sugarcane

- We use what are called Arabic numbers.

- Our decimal system came from the Middle East.

- The concept of zero was devised in India but explained and widely used in Baghdad by 800 A.D.

- The ancients calculated area and volume to design and build buildings.

- They measured circles, dividing them into degrees.

- They developed the magnetic compass.

- Although Pythagorus was Greek, research shows that the concept of the Pythagorean theorem was really discovered by the Babylonians.

- Because many people in the Middle East were merchants and traders, they had advanced banking practices, including receipts, checks (which were honored in other ancient cities), letters of credit, and simple or compound interest on loans.

- They developed the astrolabe, an instrument which tells the exact times of sunrise, sunset, and phases of the moon for any day of the year. They needed such an instrument to help them set their times of worship, their religious holidays, and the pilgrimage to Mecca that all Muslims are required to make.

- They established social science as a field of study; they were first to discuss the idea that historical events are closely related to other factors such as climate, economics, social customs, food, and religion.

- They invented musical instruments such as the lute, guitar, and tambourine.

- They made maps showing that the earth was round hundreds of years before people in the western world thought so.

- Paper making came from China but was known in Baghdad by 800 A.D.

- They had advanced ideas of public health; as early as 1000 B.C., for example, the housefly was suspected of spreading disease. By 800 A.D. they had high standards for cleanliness: for food processing, for merchants' wares, and for restaurants. They had quality control of water, with well and river water kept separate. There was also quality control of milk and dairies, to be sure milk was kept clean, pure, and undiluted.

- They developed the sexagesimal system, which uses sixty as a base. We use this in our measurement of time: 60 seconds in a minute and 60 minutes in an hour.

- They developed square numbers, numbers that form a square array because they are multiplied by themselves.

- Other mathematical concepts such as negative numbers, cubed numbers, square or cube roots, and quadratic equations

- They made many advances in medicine: accurate anatomical drawings of the eye and other parts of the body, invention of surgical instruments, professional licensing and supervision of doctors from 931 A.D. on, and the first actual account of smallpox.

- Calligraphy was first developed as an art in the Middle East.

- There were advancements in engineering, such as in well-digging and the use of underground irrigation canals with manholes.

- They made great advances in agriculture, such as what kinds of crops were suited to what soils and the introduction of new plants with medicinal or nutritional advantages: cotton, rice, mulberry trees, citrus fruits, and cherries.

Photo courtesy of Aramco World

Young children in this Middle East classroom read a story together.

16   The Code of Hammurabi

Focus

Students will learn about the world's oldest set of written laws by constructing and role-playing court cases based on laws from the *Code of Hammurabi*.

Resources

Optional costumes and props

Background

Hammurabi was the ruler of the dynasty of Babylon, a city in Mesopotamia, from 1792-1750 B.C. The Code of Hammurabi is a collection of 282 legal decisions and their extensions developed during his reign. The Code was carved (in cuneiform) on a slab of black basalt over eight feet tall.

The Code includes civil, criminal, and economic laws and was based on the concept that wrong should be punished and that this should be done uniformly throughout the kingdom. Punishment was harsh, but often compensation was given to victims of crimes. The Code shows a higher standard than the much older tribal customs in which families had waged war against one another and individuals had justified revenge for personal satisfaction. In applying the same standards to groups of individuals, the Code incorporated many elements that are considered fundamental to modern legal codes.

The Code is unusual because it is the most complete, *written* set of Babylonian laws. However, "The background of the code is a body of Sumerian law under which civilized communities had lived for many centuries. . . . Hammurabi's eminence in Mesopotamian history has long been exaggerated. It was first based on the discovery of his laws but subsequent discoveries of older, though less voluminous collections of laws have led to a less enthusiastic view. Moreover, the frequently noted resemblance between Hammurabi's laws and the Mosaic laws is now seen in terms of common heritage rather than as proof for direct dependency." (Enclopedia Britannica)

To understand the Code, students must understand that Babylonian society was divided into three distinct social classes:

- noblemen: wealthy landowners
- freemen: craftsmen, workers, and merchants
- slaves:prisoners of war, debtors, or poor men and
  women who sold themselves or their children into slavery

Teaching Tips

1. This activity has three parts. In *Part 1*, students use one or more of the sample court cases as play scripts and act them out for the rest of the class; in this way they model the procedure to be followed in *Parts 2 and 3*. In *Part 2*, groups of three to five students each select one law to dramatize; students prepare everything except the verdict; then the judge and the rest of the class decide which law applies and what the punishment—if any—should be. In *Part 3* the groups present their dramatized cases to the rest of the class, acting out the crime if time permits.

2. Decide beforehand whether or not you will assign laws to the groups or let them choose their own.

3. Be sure to file copies of the best cases written by the class, to use with future classes.

Procedure

Part 1 Readers' Theatre (See *Teaching Tips*.)

1. Have students read and act out the sample court cases as models.

Part 2 Preparing court cases

2. Divide the class into cooperative learning groups of four; give each group a copy of the Code.

3. Have each group choose a law on which to build a court case or assign a different law to each. Be sure they have paper on which to write what each person will say in court. Remind students that the defendant is the person being accused of the crime. They are to prepare everything but the verdict. Although there was no jury in Hammurabi's day and the judge would have decided the verdict and punishment (there were no juries), the class will help to decide this. (Using the scripts will help to limit the time needed for each group's case presentation.)

4. While students prepare cases, circulate to provide help and encouragement.

Part 3 Presenting the court cases (Readers' Theatre)

5. Each group presents its case to the class. At the end of each one, have the rest of the class identify the law which applies assist the judge in determining the verdict and any punishment. If time, have some groups act out their crimes.

Part 4 Summary discussion

Be sure to allow time for this; it is the most important part of the activity.

1. How are laws in the Code of Hammurabi like our laws? How are they different?

2. How much difference did it make what class the accuser belonged to? Does this happen now in our country?

3. Which do you think was the fairest of the laws presented?

4. How could we find out how much a myna of silver is?

5. What difference would it make to have a jury decide the verdict instead of a judge? In modern times, do all case have a jury trial?

Try This

1. Compare the Code with other legal systems, such as Biblical, Roman, or Islamic law. Find some and discuss them.

2. Repeat the activity using different laws from the Code.

3. Have students do further research on the Code of Hammurabi. Other laws from the Code can be found in encyclopedias and library books. (Some laws are quite brutal!)

Some Laws from the Code of Hammurabi

1. If a son has struck his father, his hands shall be cut off.

2. If a man has opened his ditch for irrigation and has been slack and caused the water to carry away his neighbor's field, he shall pay grain corresponding to the crop of the field adjoining it. If the man has no grain to reimburse, he and his goods shall be sold for silver and shall be divided among those whose grain was destroyed.

3. If a man has broken into a house, before the breach (in front of the place where he broke in) shall he be slain and there buried.

4. If a fire breaks out in a man's house, and another man has come to help extinguish it and has seen and taken property belonging to the householder, that man shall be thrown into the same fire.

5. If a builder has built a house for a man and has not made his work sound, so that the house he has made falls down and causes the death of the homeowner, that builder shall be put to death. If it causes the death of the homeowner's son, they shall kill the son of that builder. If a slave of the owner is killed, the builder shall give a slave of equal value to the owner. If goods were destroyed, the builder shall replace all that was destroyed. He shall restore the fallen house at his own cost.

6. If a boat-builder has built a boat for a man and his work is not firm, and in that same year that boat is disabled in use, then the boat-builder shall overhaul that boat and strengthen it at his own cost (with his own materials) and return the strengthened boat to the owner.

7. If a man has rented an ox, and has broken off its horn or cut off its tail or damaged its muzzle, he shall pay one quarter of its value in silver.

8. If a man has broken the bone of a nobleman, his bone shall be broken. If a man has broken the bone of a freeman, he shall pay one myna of silver. If a man has broken the bone of a man's slave, he shall pay half the value of the slave.

9. If a doctor has treated a nobleman for a severe wound and has cured the man, then he shall receive ten shekels of silver. If the patient is a freeman, the doctor shall receive five shekels of silver. If the patient is a slave, the owner of the slave shall pay the doctor two shekels of silver.

10. If a doctor has treated a noble man for a severe wound and has caused the man to die, his hand shall be cut off. If a doctor has treated a slave for a severe wound and caused him to die, he shall replace the slave with another slave of equal value.

Source: G.R. Driver and Sir J.C. Miles, The Babylonian Laws (Vol. 1), Oxford: Clarendon Press, 1952.

Sample Court Cases
from the Code of Hammurabi

Court Case #1 by Scott Zengel*

Judge: Who is standing before me?

Natiropa: I am Natiropa, a young potter. I rented my ox to this man, Riccopan, the tree-cutter. I accuse him of chopping off my ox's tail.

Riccopan: It's true, your Honor. I did rent the ox and now its tail is missing, but I didn't chop it off. The ox got its tail stuck between two trees. Before I could free it, the ox pulled its tail off.

Judge: Bring the ox over here and I will examine it. Hmm...The ox's tail has been cleanly severed. Let me check the Code of Hammurabi and I will pass judgment.

Court Case #2 by Sang Nguyen*

Judge: Who has come before me today?

Teko: I am Teko, the accuser, your honor. My son died in a boating accident. The boat was built by this man.

Judge: And who are you?

Tomat: I am Tomat, the boat builder.

Judge: Tomat, why did you sell a bad boat?

Tomat: I needed money to feed my family. I intended to fix the boat as soon as I had some extra materials.

Judge: Teko, did you lose any merchandise when the boat sank?

Teko: Yes, Two of my slaves died and I lost five containers of barley. My arm was broken when I tried to stop the boat from sinking...

Judge: This will be a difficult judgment. I'd better check the Code of Hammurabi before I decide what to do.

Court Case #3 by Grant Johnstone*

Judge: What seems to be the problem with you two men?

Lukani: That man is responsible for my son's death!

Mirte: You're a liar! Why I ought to...!

Judge: You both better stop it before I have your lips cut off! Who is the accuser?

Lukani: I am. My name is Lukani. One year ago, I hired this man to build me a house. Less than two weeks after he finished, pieces of the ceiling began to fall down. Two days ago, the whole house collapsed and killed my son. I demand justice!

Judge: Defendant, what can you say to defend yourself?

Mirte: I am Mirte, the builder. I am a very busy man. I simply didn't have time to repair the house. He could have fixed it himself.

Judge: I think the Code of Hammurabi can help me solve this case. Let me check...

* All three authors are sixth-grade students in the Manchester GATE Program, Fresno Unified School District.

17   Making Cuneiform Tablets

Focus

Students will create cuneiform tablets to learn about writing in ancient Mesopotamia.

Resources

For each student:
>   air-dry clay, size of golf ball (5 pounds for 30 students)
>   plasticene modeling clay (for practicing, same amount)
>   dowel - 6-inch piece, 1/4-1/2" diameter (see *Teaching Tips*)
>   waxed paper

Background
(See the resource sheet *The History of Writing.)*

Guidelines

1. CAUTION: Work quickly with the air-dry clay, because it will begin to dry and harden after 10 minutes. Depending on temperature and humidity, complete drying can take one to two days. Baking the tablets in an oven will speed up the process. (Follow instructions on the package.)

2. For styluses, the ancient Mesopotamians used the reeds that grew along the Tigris and Euphrates Rivers; if you have access to reeds, these would make the most authentic styluses. Shaped dowels also work well. Craft sticks or even pencils may also be used, although it is harder to obtain the wedge-shaped marks. *Procedure* directions assume the use of dowel.

3. Beforehand or with students, make up cuneiform equivalents for the letters of our alphabet, so students can print their names on the tablets. This won't be authentic, but will give students some experience using cuneiform.

Procedure

1. Distribute the pieces of dowel.
2. Students make one end of their dowels wedge-shaped by rubbing them on cement, sandpaper, or a file. Poking the stylus straight into clay should leave a triangular imprint. Tipping the stylus to the side and dragging it adds the tail.

3. Distribute pieces of waxed paper and hunks of practice clay.

4. Flatten the clay ball to form a tablet one-half-inch thick.

5. Practice poking the stylus into the clay. Then try making some characters shown on the fact sheet. You may also want to let students try drawing pictures in the clay.

6. Have students decide what to write on the final tablet. Practice enough that they can work quickly on the air-dry clay. Collect the practice clay and distribute the air-dry clay. Have them write in cuneiform and identify tablets with names or initials.

7. Set the tablets aside to dry.

8. Share impressions and questions about the activity:

   - What do you think were the advantages of cuneiform writing as compared to the pictures people had drawn before that?
   - What were the disadvantages of cuneiform writing and tablets?
   - Who invented cuneiform writing?
   - What was used as a stylus to do the original Sumerian cuneiform writing?
   - How is cuneiform writing different from ours? [one symbol does not stand for one letter or one sound]

Try This

1. Compare the cuneiform writing of ancient Mesopotamia with Egyptian hieroglyphics.

2. Make up an alphabet using cuniform characters. Have students write their names in the new alphabet!

Cuniform Tablets

and Cylinder Seals

18   The History of Writing
Resource Sheet

Long ago, people passed along information by oral tradition. They told their children stories again and again, so that the children would remember. When the children grew up, they told the same stories to their children. Oral tradition is still an important way of preserving history, especially in places where the language has not yet been written down or where few can read.

To make a more lasting record, ancient people painted pictures of important events or just what life was like. Scientists have discovered cave paintings (mostly of animals) that were done thousands of years ago. When people wanted to tell longer stories with their pictures, they made them smaller and used simple outline pictures of objects (pictographs). The hieroglyphics of Egypt and the early cuneiform of Sumer are good examples.

As people told stories with pictures, they used symbols to express feelings or ideas. A drawing of the sun was used as the symbol for *day* or *heat*, rather than just as the sun itself. For *war* or *fight*, they might picture a stick man with a spear or bow and arrow. For *sad,* they might picture an eye with a tear.

Eventually the symbols looked less and

less like the objects and ideas they represented. In classic cuneiform, for example, a wooden or clay tool called a stylus was used to produce wedge-shaped indentations. These symbols were put together to form complete words, thoughts, or sentences. This sound-writing was developed over a period of hundreds or even thousands of years.

Alphabets are the most advanced developments in writing. The ancient Babylonians used cuneiform with 350 different symbols. Imagine learning 350 symbols instead of the 26 in our alphabet!

Although one alphabet may be used for the written form of several languages, that does not mean people who speak those

Original Pictographs	Early Cuneiform	Classic Cuneiform	Meaning
			bird
			fish
			ox

languages can understand each other. For example, our Roman alphabet is used to write English and French, but we do not automatically understand French when it is either written or spoken. The same thing is true of the Arabic alphabet; people in Iran use the same alphabet as those in Saudi Arabia, but they speak totally different languages. In the Hebrew alphabet, only consonant sounds are used, and the reader supplies all of the vowels.

About two hundred years ago, some explorers became interested in finding out more about life long ago. They went to the Middle East and dug down into some small hills. They soon found the ruins of an ancient Assyrian palace. Everyone was very excited, because pottery and other things they found could tell them a lot about the life of the people who lived there. Hard clay tablets that were tossed into a pile of trash were later found to contain *cuneiform,* called that because the Latin word *cuneus* means *wedge.* This was an important discovery, because it helped us learn much about the life and history of the ancient people who lived in that area.

Originally, the people drew pictures, but this was hard to do in the wet clay. This may have been why they started using styluses. In the chart on page 107, notice that the stylus could be pressed in two different ways, with and without the tail, and also facing in several different directions.

Materials used for writings became more and more portable, from the walls of caves, to clay tablets, to papyrus, and then to more advanced types of paper. Gradually written communication became more and more important to peoples of the ancient world.

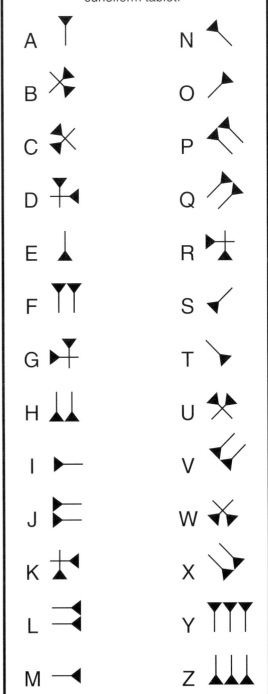

MODIFIED CUNEIFORM ALPHABET
The cuneiform characters used by the ancient writers of Mesopotamia was very complicated. Here is a simplified set of characters that you can use to create your cuneiform tablet.

19   Making Cylinder Seals

The Focus

Students will learn how ancient Mesopotamians made and used cylinder seals as a distinctive signature.

Resources

For each student:

For Part 1:
air-dry clay, the size of a golf ball (3 pounds for 30 students) (see *Teaching Tips*)
plasticene clay for <u>practice,</u> same quantity
waxed paper
dowel stylus (see *Making Cuneiform Tablets*)
pencil or straightened paper clip (see *Teaching Tips*)

For Part 2:
air-dry clay, the size of tennis ball (5 pounds for 30 students)
waxed paper
pencil
dowel stylus

Background

Some of the most interesting artifacts found in the archeological excavations of ancient Mesopotamia are the cylinder seals. Each small cylinder of carved stone or fired clay was carved with a unique set of symbols or pictures that belonged to its owner. When the cylinder seal was rolled across a damp piece of clay, it left a unique rectangular imprint. Kings and other important officials "signed" cuneiform tablets to prove who was really sending the message.

Teaching Tips

1. In *Part 1*, students make the cylinder seals and set them aside to dry for two days. Two days later, in *Part 2*, students *write* their signatures with the seals by rolling them on a clay tablet like the one used in *Making Cuneiform Tablets.*

2. Beforehand, follow the directions to make a cylinder seal to use as a model. Those shown in lesson 18 are about 3 cm long and 2 cm in diameter.

3. After the seal has dried, details can be sharpened using a straightened paper clip.

Procedure

Part 1 Making the cylinder seals

1. Use your model seal to explain its general construction and use. Review procedures for working with air-dry clay given in the previous lesson.

2. Have students design their seals, reminding them names and messages should be reversed, so that they will print correctly.

3. Distribute waxed paper, golf-ball-sized piece of practice clay, and styluses. Roll practice clay into a cylinder shape with flat ends. Using the stylus and pencil or paper clip, carve the design on the practice seal.

4. Distribute air-dry clay and make final cylinder seals. Set aside to dry.

Part 2 (Two days later)

1. Distribute seals and paper clips. Sharpen detail on seals.

2. Distribute tablet-sized pieces of clay and waxed paper.

3. Flatten the clay on the waxed paper to make a flat tablet wider than the seal's circumference. Roll the cylinder seal across the clay to make an imprint. Set the tablet aside to dry.

4. Discuss how cylinder seals were used:

   • In ancient times, how were cylinder seals a step of progress?

   • What would be the advantages and disadvantages of using cylinder seals?

   • What were some of the similarities and difference among the seals made by members of the class?

   • What are some devices in modern times that have uses similar to those of cylinder seals? [branding irons, signatures, credit cards]

Try This

1. Investigate other ways in which ancient people left their marks. [Egyptian hieroglyphics on pillars or obelisks].

2. Discuss how people throughout history have "left their mark," (coat of arms, trademark, brand, norary public seal, and so on).

3. Make cylinder seals with some modern trade marks on them.

20   Settling Disputes

Focus

By simulation and real-life application, students will learn and practice settling individual, local group, and international disputes.

Resources

Part 1 (for each group):
  Process Sheet

Part 2 (for each group):
  Process sheet

Part 3 (for each group):
  Map
  Information Sheet
  Process Sheet

Part 4 (for each group):
  Clippings about international disputes
  (from newspapers or newsmagazines)
  Process Sheet

Background

Conflicts happen when people or groups or nations disagree on some issue. Whether the issue is first place in the lunch line or which nation should have control over a certain territory, it needs to be recognized as a difference which needs to be settled. Conflicts are normal and inevitable; what is difficult is the resolving of conflicts so that the solution meets the needs of both sides.

The first step is to describe the dispute. Although people usually assume they know what the dispute is, it is often enlightening when the dispute must be stated in written form. For this reason this is the first step to be taken in each dispute in this activity.

Some disputes have clear right and wrong sides. If a girl is walking along a school hallway and another girl hits her <u>for no reason</u>, the girl who does the hitting is wrong. There is no need for a discussion or cooperative problem solving. In the same illustration, however, if we find out the first girl took the attacker's purse yesterday, the picture changes and becomes more complex; here both did something wrong. Therefore, the second step in each activity is to be sure that right and wrong actions are identified and placed in proper sequence.

In most disputes, however, there is not a clear right or wrong. The damage may have been done with words, so it is difficult, impossible, or perhaps pointless to go back to construct exact events in sequence. The larger the number of people involved, the more difficult it becomes to settle the matter. People tend to continue arguing or fighting or killing unless someone or something helps them realize it is to their advantage to stop. To settle the matter once and for all, expressing both—or all—points of view must take place. This usually takes time, but it is essential.

Although the process we have adopted may appear complicated at first , it will be effective, but only if students use it again and again so the process becomes part of their behavior. All of the steps are important, and they must be followed every time. The ultimate goal with students is to have them use it automatically in their daily lives.

There are three basic ways that most disputes are resolved: force, authority, or creative problem solving. (1) **Force** may be defined as yelling, threatening, or fighting. It is characterized by those on one side (or both sides) of the dispute insisting on getting their way. (2) With **authority**, the solution is provided by a person or a system of rules or laws, with or without the wholehearted agreement of both parties; force may be used to enforce the solution or verdict and prevent greater harm. (3) In **creative problem solving**, the two sides are involved in negotiations to create a solution that satisfies both sides; compromises are often involved.

There are advantages and disadvantages to all three strategies. With force, the side that settles the matter with force considers the situation solved—often quickly—and for them the matter is settled. In reality, the matter is not really settled at all, although it may sometimes look that way on the surface. One side forces a solution, but that means there is a winner and a loser; the loser may give in but often starts thinking immediately of a way to turn the tables and become the ultimate winner. The minute this happens, the winner that has become the loser repeats the process, seeking to become the winner again. This repeated retaliation takes place in gang conflicts, organized crime, and wars between nations, but also in many everyday settings; the key is that one side perceives itself as the loser, the powerless person or group. It is easy—and human—to retain grudges and hostilities with a righteous attitude that one has been wronged. This becomes a problem, especially when there is a plan for retaliation or revenge. The perpetuation of the problem usually prevents a permanent solution.

The use of authority also has advantages and disadvantages. First, it is meant to provide a solution with no one being physically hurt. In sports, when two players disagree, the umpire or referee (the authority) makes a ruling, fault and punishment are determined, and the game goes on. Second, decisions are supposed to be based on who is right, rather than who is stronger. When adults disagree about who caused a car accident, they tell the police and the insurance company; if they still disagree, they may take their conflict to court, another level of authority. The judge listens to both sides and decides who is right according to the traffic laws and the evidence. One disadvantage is that the fairness which is intended may not always be carried through. For example, poor people often feel that they are at a disadvantage in a court because they cannot afford expensive lawyers. A second disadvantage is that the settling of the dispute may take a long time; the uncertainty and the expense of court cases may cause one or both parties to try to settle the problem in other ways. A third disadvantage is that there is no guarantee that when the solution is given, it will be fair. In a civilized society, however, most people and groups abide by the decisions which are given.

The third strategy, creative problem solving, is the most difficult to manage but is assumed by many to be the most satisfactory in many types of situations. The key is to bring the two sides together and work out a solution in which both sides can perceive themselves as winners. A good example of this procedure is constructive labor negotiations, when the two sides meet (often with a mediator that both sides consider neutral) and face the reality that they must find a settlement in which both groups feel they have been dealt with fairly. The arbitrator does not impose the settlement but promotes communication and understanding.

In many disputes we cannot choose which strategy to use. For example, we are excluding from consideration the emergency situations when force or authority may be the only sensible solution. When a child runs into the street and refuses to move, you have to grab him or her before a car comes along; you do not have time to stop and discuss the matter. Most of the time, however, there is time to resolve the conflict in more thoughtful ways.

Photo courtesy of Aramco World

Teaching Tips

1. For each of the four parts of the activity, the class should be divided into cooperative learning groups of four students each. Roles will be facilitator, timer, reporter, and encourager. (See the chapter on *Teaching Skills and Strategies* for help in using this strategy.) At the end of each part of the activity, decide whether or not to keep students in the same groups for the next part.

2. The activity leads students to deal with disputes on three levels, individual, local group, and international. Because international issues are so complex, a simulated dispute has been inserted; the goal of this activity is to avoid any possible prejudices so that students can concentrate on the peace process itself.

   Part 1: Disputes between individuals
   Part 2: Local group disputes (family, club, and school issues)
   Part 3: Simulated international dispute
   Part 4: Real-life international diputes (selected by teacher)

3. This whole activity, as with social science in general, is meant to empower students to evaluate world problems and consider effective solutions. As students apply repeatedly the

procedure for analyzing problem situations, it is hoped that they will recognize reactions they have observed or experienced and will discard solutions that they realize are inappropriate. Of course the ultimate test will be students' application of the process to real-life problems after the activity is over!

4. In *Part 3*, the class will be divided into four groups, three countries and the international peacekeeping organization, the *Federation of Nations (FON)*. If possible, arrange the classroom (desks) according to the map, with *FON* desks off to the side. If this is not convenient, at least have students change places so that members of each group are together. Decide whether groups will discuss both crises at once or one crisis at a time.

5. Beforehand, you should plan possible problems for the second dispute of *Parts 1* and *3* and the problems to use for *Part 4.*

Procedure

Part 1 Individual disputes

1. Discuss why people have differences of opinion, using as examples incidents that have happened recently within and outside of the classroom.

2. Divide the class into groups and define roles. Then read this first problem with the whole class:

> Bob and Jose were best friends until Luke's family moved into the neighborhood. Since Bob and Luke were in the same classes, it was easy for them to start doing things together. Jose was hurt, being left out much of the time. Bob and Jose couldn't find some things he was sure he had put there. When Jose complained to Bob, he wouldn't listen; Bob thought Jose was unfair, not wanting to share the locker. One day Jose saw Luke dumping a pile of books and notebooks into the locker. Now he wouldn't be able to find anything. He was very angry.

3. Distribute one Process Sheet to each group. Explain that each group will work through the Process Sheet. <u>Stress that everyone in a group must agree to an answer before it is written down by the reporter.</u>

4. When all groups have finished, discuss the results as a whole class. Students may have strong opinions about what is right or what is best.

5. Now divide into groups again and think of an individual dispute known to one of the group. Use another copy of the

process sheet to analyze the dispute. (With older students, you can use blank paper, using the process sheet as a pattern.)

6. Try to allow time to have reporters share these dispute analyses and solutions; this is where much of the real learning of the concepts will take place.

Part 2 Local group disputes

1. Although this type of dispute may arise in a family, sports team, or club, we recommend using here a school issue in which all students are interested. Choose a simple one, such as whether or not hats should be worn indoors or whether disruptive students should be excluded from riding the school bus; choose an issue on which there are clearly two sides with some students willing to adopt both opinions. Decide whether or not all groups will analyze the same problem.

2. Divide into groups. Groups follow the process sheet in describing, analyzing, and finding solutions to the problem given. <u>Remind students that everyone in the group must agree to an answer before it is written down.</u>

Photo courtesy of Aramco World

3. In a whole-class discussion, have reporters share their results. Discuss any issues about which students feel strongly. If possible, have an administrator visit so students can express their concern and suggest possible solutions.

Part 3 Description of situation

1. Assign students to the four groups, the three countries and the *FON*). Students need to agree to adopt the point of view for group to which they are assigned; they will retain their roles throughout this part of the activity.

2. Display the transparency of the map. Be sure students understand that the nations and the *FON* are imaginary, but the *FON* is like the United Nations; discuss the purpose and powers of the *UN* if students are not familiar with it. Stress that this dispute is based on real issues that have caused serious problems for hundreds of years; many wars have been fought because people could not settle similar problems peacefully.

3. Distribute the resource sheets to the groups. Read and discuss the *Background* section separately. Help students to picture life in all three countries.

4. Distribute a map and two process sheets to each group; all groups will analyze both crises. Discuss the present situation as a whole class or in groups. Actually there are two crises; you may prefer to declare that they will deal with one of the problems at a time. When you deal with the invasion of Victa,

have some of the students vacate their desks while some from Angra move into those seats.

5. Have all groups discuss how they feel to develop some emotional commitment. You may even want them to write it down. For example, the Vegans might say, "Angra, you sent in your soldiers and took our land. Some of our people have no homes or farms now. We demand you give us back our land."

6. Have groups use the process sheets to analyze the disputes. As they do, encourage action, such as meetings of Vega or Mega with the *FON*. Have whole-class discussions whenever this seems to be productive. Be sure the reporter from each group is the only spokesperson.

7. The simulation is over when all groups have agreed upon the solutions, which are usually compromises. If you must call time, remind students that some international disputes are ongoing.

Part 4 Actual international dispute

1. Using the clippings, list and discuss some current international disputes.

2. Have each group choose a dispute to process. Use additional copies of the process sheets again to find possible solutions.

Photo courtesy of Aramco World

Settling Disputes
Information Sheet for Part 3

Background

There are three countries and the Federation of Nations or FON, the international peacekeeping organization.

With its long shoreline, it is not surprising that much of Mega's life and economy has been based on the sea. There are three major seaports, with international trade and commercial fishing the major industries. There is also some dairy farming inland on the rolling hills. The Megans work hard, and many of them are well-educated.

Victa is a small country with no coastline at all. Farming is the major industry. On the fertile plains the people raise mostly wheat and also some fruits and vegetables. On the rolling hills in the east, there is some dairy farming. The people are peaceful and live in small towns. Whenever there has been a war in the area, Victa has always been neutral.

Angra is the largest of the three countries. It is overpopulated, and there is not much fertile land for farming. The southern border of Angra is too rocky for a harbor. Angra gets much of its food from Victa, along with fish from Mega. Angrans ship and receive manufactured goods through the seaport in Mega. Angrans maintain a strong standing army. In recent years, countries bordering Angra on the north and east have become very powerful; they have taken over part of Angra, including some large coal mines, some fertile farmland, and a mountain area with a lot of tourist business.

The Federation of Nations (FON) is an international organization with headquarters in the city closest to you. All three countries are members and have ambassadors there.

The Present Crisis

Six months ago, Angra invaded Victa and took over a section of it, claiming it really belonged to them anyway. This will provide some farmland and space for Angrans to live. Victa has complained to the *FON* about this invasion.

The Angrans pay customs fees to Mega for all of the goods shipped in and out through the seaports. Recently Mega has raised these fees (again), and Agrans have refused to pay the additional money. Instead they have sent soldiers on the trains to the seaports. They have also stationed a large number of soldiers along the southeast Megan border. The Megans think Angra is getting ready to invade this area and take over a seaport.

Mega and Victa have complained to the FON. Mega supports Victa's complaint and Victa supports Mega's complaint. Other countries in the area do not want to get involved.

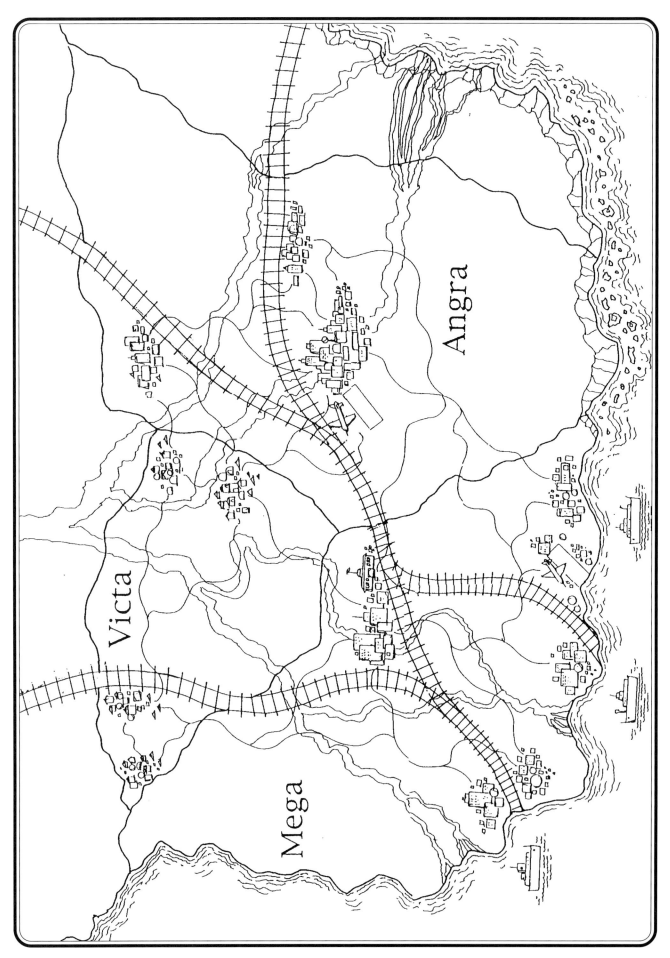

Angra

Victa

Mega

Names: Facilitator _____   Reporter _____

Timer _____   Encourager _____

Settling Disputes
Process Sheet

1.   What is the dispute? _____

_____

_____

2.   What are the two (or more) sides of the dispute, the points of view?

_____

_____

3.   Is one side <u>clearly</u> right? (If there is any discussion, the answer is "no!")

❑ yes   ❑ no

4.   Has there been damage, theft, or personal injury? _____

_____

5.   Name three ways this problem might be settled in real life:

By force _____

_____

By authority _____

_____

By creative problem solving _____

_____

6.   Of these, what seems to be the best solution and why? _____

_____

21 Resource List

Addresses for Specific Countries:

United Nations
Room S-994
New York 10017
Free information on history of the Israeli-Palestin-
ian dispute

Cultural Division
Embassy of the State of Bahrai
3502 International Dr., N.W.
Washington, D.C. 20008

Permanent Mission of Iraq to the U.N.
14 East 79th St.
New York, NY 10021

Israeli Government Tourist Office
350 Fifth Avenue
New York City, NY 10118

Jordan Information Bureau
2319 Wyoming Ave., N.W.
Washington, D.C. 20004

Permanent Mission of Kuwait to the U.N.
321 East 44th St.
New York, NY 10017

League of Arab States
747 Third Avenue
New York City, NY 10017
Pamphlets, especially on Arab civilization.

Consulate General of Lebanon
9 East 76th St.
New York, NY 10021

Embassy of the Sultanate of Oman
2342 Massachusetts Ave., NW
Washington, D.C. 20008

Permanent Mission of Oman to the U.N.
866 United Nations Plaza, Suite 540
New York, NY 10017

Permanent Mission of Qatar to the U.N.
747 Third Ave., 22nd Floor
New York, NY 10017

Palestine Affairs Center
1730 K Street, Suite 70-3
Washington, DC NW 20006

Embassy of the Kingdom of Saudi Arabia
601 New Hampshire Ave., NW
Washington, D.C. 20037

Permanent Mission of Syria to the U.N.
820 Second Ave., Suite 1000
New York, NY 10017

Turkish Government Tourism and Information
Office
821 U.N. Plaza
New York City, NY 10017

Permanent Mission of the United Arab Emirates to
the U.N.
747 Third Ave.
New York, NY 10017

Permanent Mission of the Peoples Democratic
Republic of Yemen to the U.N.
413 East 51st St.
New York, NY 10022

Often an office of tourism or a commercial source
is more helpful than an embassy or a consulate.
Your local library, reference desk, should have the
latest edition of the State Department list of
Foreign Consular Offices in the United States.
This publication also lists addresses of tourism
offices throughout the United States. Your local
tourist agencies may have travel brochures and
posters. Airlines based in Middle East countries
may also have helpful information.

Sources for Publications, Information, and Supplies:

AWAIR
1400 Shattuck Avenue, Suite 9
Berkeley, CA 94709
Phone: (510) 704-0517
K-12 materials, including *The Arab World Notebook*,
secondary level (a thorough resource collection
covering many topics such as history, women,
food, and so on, useful for any level, cost about
$40.); *The Arabs: Activities for the Elementary School
Level;* and storybooks about Arab children and
young people.

Aramco World
Box 469008
Escondido, CA 92046-9008
Free subscription to this beautifully illustrated
magazine available to readers with an interest in
Saudi Arabia or Islamic culture.

California Geographic Alliance
Dept. of Geography, CSUC
Chico, CA 95929-0425
Maps and curriculum resources.

Center for Middle East Studies
University of California at Berkeley
Berkeley, CA 94720
Phone: (510)642-8208

Choices Education Project
Center for Foreign Policy Development
Brown University, Box 1948
Providence, RI 02912-9914
Publishes topical, reproducible curricula on
foreign policy issues for grades 9-12, including
study guides and maps; some could be adapted
for lower grades. Write for publications list.

Congressional Quarterly, Inc.
1414 22nd Street, NW
Washington, DC 20037
Pamphlet titled *The Middle East.*

Educators for Social Responsibility
23 Garden Street
Cambridge, MA 02138
Materials on conflict resolution.

Jewish Community Relations Council
121 Steuart Street, Suite 301
San Francisco, CA 94105
Phone: (415) 957-1551
Fax: (415) 979-0981
Publishes excellent curriculum project titled
*Nationalism in the Middle East - A Case Study: Israel
and Syria,* appropriate for secondary students.

Laguna Clay Co.
14400 Lomitas Ave.
Industry, CA 91746
Sells air-dry or fire-clay for cuneiform tablets and
cylinder seals.

Middle East Research and Information Project
1500 Massachusetts Ave., NW, Suite 119
Washington, DC 20005
Its publications focus on contemporary Middle
East problems such as human rights, religious
freedom, and women's rights: for teachers and
advanced students.

National Geographic Society
P.O. Box 98018
Washington, D.C. 20090
Phone: (1-800) 368-2728
Monthly periodical and other publications often
include articles and maps related to Middle East;
when reading level too high, suggest using
illustrations with simplified captions.

Palestine Liberation Organization
115 65th Street
New York City, NY 10017
Phone: (212) 288-8500
Newspaper Palestine Focus plus other political
information.
Resource Center for Non-Violence
515 Broadway
Santa Cruz, CA 95060
Phone: (408) 423-1626
Produces Middle East Study Packet

Professional Development Division
Fresno Pacific College
1717 South Chestnut Avenue
Fresno, CA 93702
Phone: (209) 453-2015
Fax: (209) 453-
Offers in-service courses on a variety of subjects
including Middle East.

Third World Resources - Data Center
464 19th Street
Oakland, CA 94612
Phone: (510) 835-4692
Quarterly review, many sources, sample $2.

World Almanac
The current edition is available at libraries and
newsstands.

Bibliography

Abercrombie, T. J. (1991). Ibn Battuta, Prince of Travelers. *The National Geographic Magazine,* 180:6:2-49.

Bauman, E., Johnson, W., Peck, I. (1986). *The Ancient World.* New York: Scholastic.

Canby, T. Y. (1991). After the Storm. *The National Geographic Magazine,* 180:2:2-35.

Du Ry, C. J. (1969). *Art of the Ancient, Near, and Middle East.* New York: Harry N. Abrams, Inc.

Earle, S.A. (1992). Persian Gulf Pollution. *The National Geographic Magazine,* 181:2:122-134.

Esler, A. (1986). *The Human Adventure.* Englewood Cliffs, NJ: Prentice-Hall.

Everyday Life in Bible Times (1990). Washington, DC: National Geographic Society.

Garraty, J. A., Gay, P. (Eds.) (1972).*Colombia History of the World.* New York: Harper & Row.

Hoffman, Y. (1989). *The World of the Bible for Young Readers.* New York: Viking Kestrel.

King, L. W. (1919). *History of Babylon.* London: Chatto & Windus.

Lillys, W., Reiff, R., Esin, E. (1965). *Oriental Miniatures: Persian, Indian, Turkish.* Rutland, VT: Charles E. Tuttle.

Logan, R. K. (1986). *The Alphabet Effect.* New York: Morrow.

Nawwab, I. I., Speers, P. C., Hoye, P. F. (Eds.) (1981). *Aramco and Its World.* Dharan, Saudi Arabia: Aramco.

Ober, J. H. (1965). *Writing: Man's Greatest Invention.* Baltimore: Peabody Institute.

Pallis, S. A., (1956). *Antiquity of Iraq.* Copenhagen: Ejner Munksgaard.

Saggs, H. W. F. (1989). *Civilization Before Greece and Rome.* New Haven: Tale.

Saggs, H. W. F. (1962). *Greatness That Was Babylon.* New York: Hawthorne Books.

Severy, M. (1990). Iraq: Crucible of Civilization. *The National Geographic Magazine,* 179: 5:102-115.

Severy, M. (1987). The World of Suleyman the Magnificent. *The National Geographic Magazine,* 172:5:552-601.

Shabbas, A., Al-Qazzaz, A. (Eds.) (1989). *Arab World Notebook..* Berkeley:AWAIR (see above section for address).

Szulc, T. (1992). Who Are the Palestinians. *The National Geographic Magazine,* 181:6:84-113.

Time Frame Series. (1988). Alexandria, VA: Time-Life Books.

-*The Age of the God-Kings, 3000-1500 B.C.*
-*Barbarian Tides, 1500-600 B.C.*
-*A Soaring Spirit, 600-400 B.C.*
-*Empires Ascendant, 400 B.C.-200 A.D*
-*Empires Beseiged, 200-600 A.D.*

Vesilind, P. J. (1993). The Middle East's Water, Critical Resource. *The National Geographic Magazine,* 183:5:38-71.

Wood, A. (1987) *Being a Jew.* London: B.T. Batsford.

Wood, A. (1987). *Being a Muslim.* London: B.T. Batsford.

World Almanac (1992). New York:Pharos.

Photo courtesy of Aramco World

22   Maps and Atlases

Biblical Archaeology Review
P.O. Box 7026
Red Oak, IA 51591-2026
Bimonthly periodical, often includes articles of interest to groups studying the Middle East.

Hammond, Inc.
515 Valley St.,
Maplewood, NJ 17040
Publishes *Atlas of the Middle East* (1991) with information on geography, history, and languages. and other useful maps.

National Geographic Society
P.O. Box 98018
Washington, D.C. 20090
Monthly periodical includes maps; check the index at your library.

Nystrom
3333 Elston Avenue
Chicago, IL 60618-5898
Publishes a combination political/geophysical map of Middle East (1993), available as wall map or laminated smaller version with rainfall, population, growing seasons, and land use; includes Turkey.

Rand McNally
Educational Publishing Division
P.O. Box 1906
Skokie, IL 60667-8906
The *Classroom Atlas* (1992) includes a limited amount of information on the Middle East. The *Historical Atlas of the World* (1991) is useful, especially to advanced students. Laminated map does not include Turkey.

U.S. Army Reserve
1815 North Fort Meyer Drive, Room 501
Arlington, VA 22209-1805
May offer wall maps free.

World Eagle, Inc.
64 Washburn Avenue
Wellesley, MA 02181
(617) 235-1415
Publishes world and regional outline maps including perspective maps such as Middle East as seen from Israel.

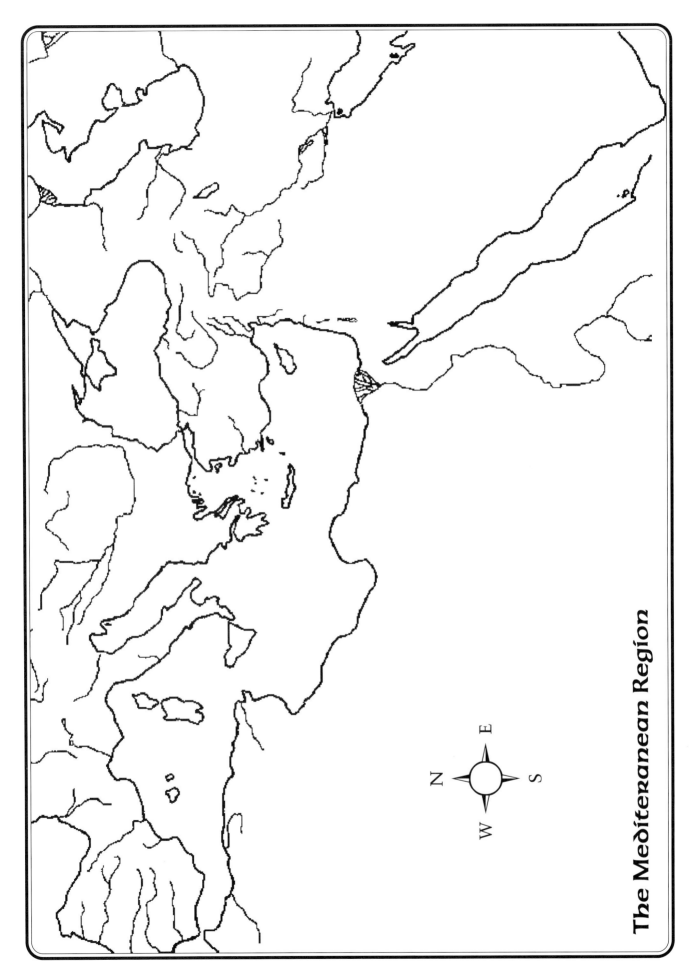

The Mediteranean Region

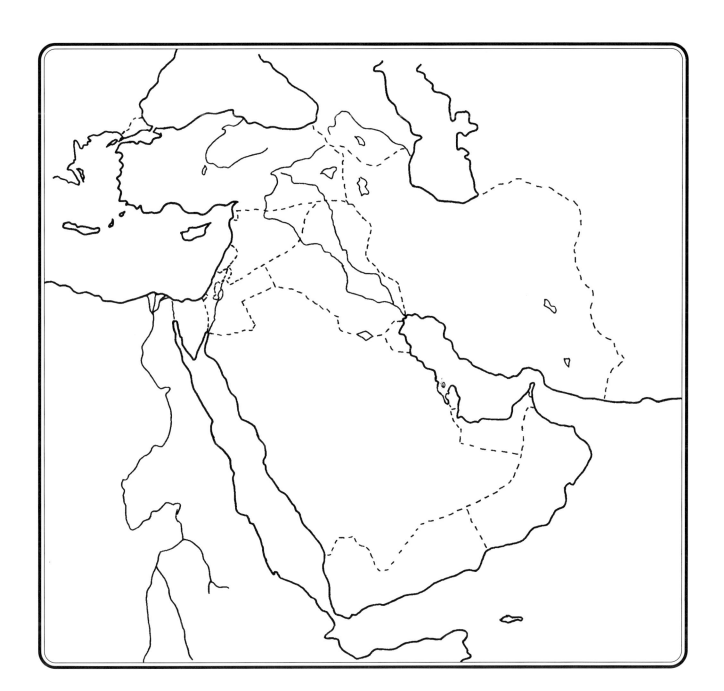

Middle East

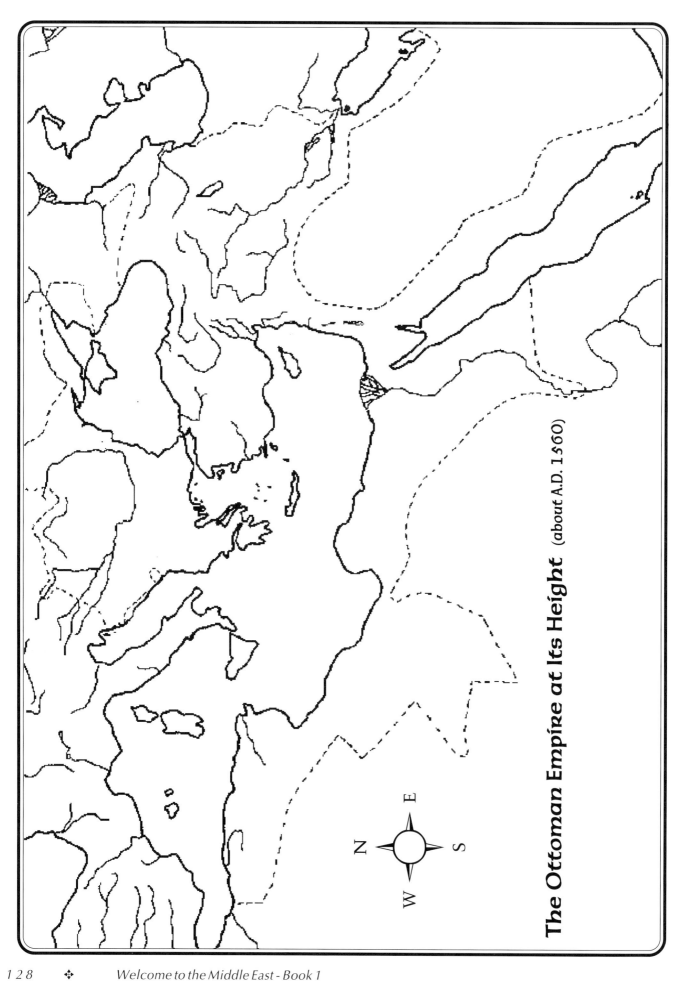

The Ottoman Empire at Its Height (about A.D. 1560)

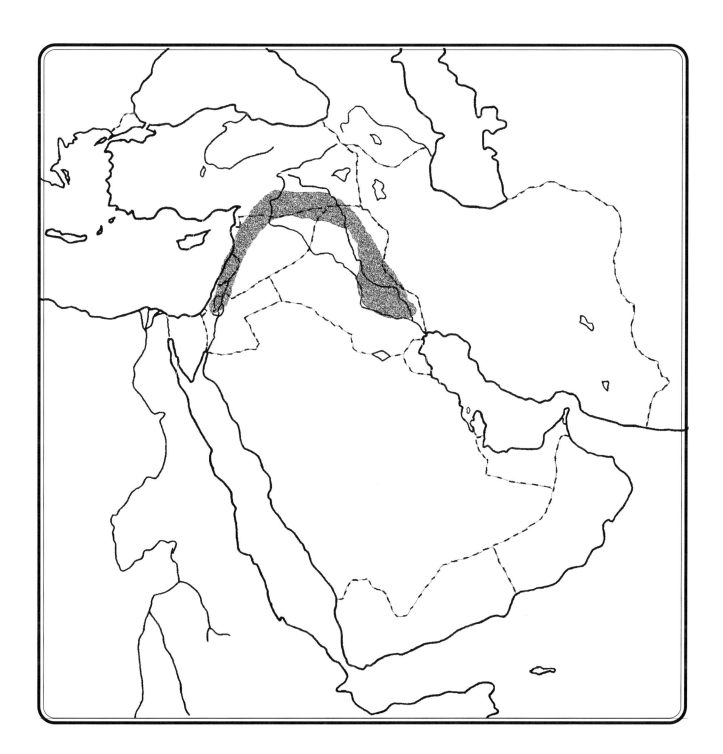

The Fertile Crescent